Handling Hot Coffee

Preventing Spills, Burns, and Lawsuits

DAN COX

Handling
Hot Coffee

Preventing Spills,
Burns, and Lawsuits

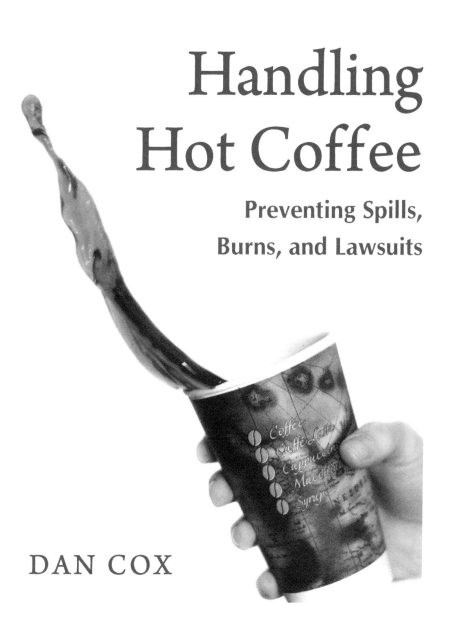

DAN COX

Published by
Red Barn Books of Vermont
An imprint of Wind Ridge Books
Shelburne, Vermont 05482

Handling Hot Coffee
Preventing Spills, Burns, and Lawsuits

Photographs by Julia Luckett
Cover and book design by Laurie Thomas

ISBN: 978-1-935922-24-7

Published by Red Barn Books of Vermont
An imprint of Wind Ridge Books of Vermont, LLC
P. O. Box 636
Shelburne, Vermont 05482

Printed in the United States of America

Contents

Chapter 3
Preventive Measures: Warnings and Spill Reactions

Chapter 4
Brew and Sue: Hot Beverage Litigation

Preface

I prepared and wrote this manual to make a comprehensive reference guide available to the coffee and hot beverage industry that would provide validation and clarification of temperature standards in the context of hot beverage litigation and would serve to help retail establishments prepare a defense if sued. Previously, the industry and its lawyers lacked a single resource in which the pertinent, diverse, but related subjects—food science, biology, medicine, and litigation—were compiled. That is the purpose of this manual.

Over the course of my career, I have been involved in the coffee industry in several professional capacities and am currently the owner of Coffee Enterprises, the largest independent coffee laboratory in the US. This work also has allowed me to keep abreast of industry issues and changes in brewing and serving equipment with regard to coffee quality, customer satisfaction, and consumer safety. I became interested in the burn/spill litigation process in 1999 when retained as an expert witness and I have continued to serve in that role in many subsequent cases involving industry standards and the temperatures required to brew coffee.

In *Handling Hot Coffee,* my colleagues and I have compiled and condensed relevant hot beverage litigation information into four content areas: (1) industry standards for brewing, serving, and storing hot beverages (2) information on burns and the burn risk of hot beverages (3) prevention of spills and warning psychology (4) lessons from past litigation, liability, and defense strategies.

In the first section of this manual, industry standards and research are discussed and explanations given for the necessity of certain brewing and holding temperatures. These are not personal opinions, but are widely established and accepted industry standards. In the sections on burns, preventing spills and burns, and hot beverage litigation, I have offered my opinions and recommendations, which are not agreed upon by everyone in the hot beverage industry, nor are they industry standards.

Ideally, we hope that the millions of daily hot coffee and tea drinking customers neither spill their cups nor are they burned. Additionally, we hope that no company is sued … but if that does happen, may this manual prove to be a supportive professional resource. May it also serve to contribute to burn knowledge, and most importantly, spill prevention.

Dan Cox

Introduction

Hot coffee is brewed, purchased, dispensed, and handled millions of times every day. Cups are lidded and un-lidded, sugar added, cream poured, to-go trays juggled, and drive-thru windows navigated. Sleep-deprived parents press their coffee makers on, Keurig cups keep people happy in waiting rooms, over-caffeinated students line up for their fifth cup of the day, and harried baristas juggle taking orders, making change, and pouring drinks. Most of the time, the resulting beverages are enjoyable. But sometimes the coffee is too cold. Sometimes the besieged barista gives out regular instead of decaf. And sometimes people spill coffee. Very occasionally, those spills result in scald burns. And sometimes people sue their coffee purveyors.

Did lawsuits over spilled hot coffee really start with Liebeck v. McDonald's in 1994? This famous product liability case became the flashpoint for seemingly frivolous lawsuits. The $2,860,000 that Mrs. Liebeck was originally awarded seemed outrageous. Even when the amount was reduced to $640,000 upon appeal, the dollar figure appeared excessive. Is our culture crazy? She spilled coffee on herself and admitted it!

The Liebeck case, no matter how you feel about tort reform, became the tipping point for McDonald's. The reality is this: prior to Liebeck, and in addition to the "Golden Arches," many other food service retailers have been sued because of harmful burns caused when customers spilled hot coffee, tea, cocoa, or water. When consumers spill hot liquids in their own homes and are burned, a lawsuit usually does not occur; however, when hot liquids are purchased in a commercial establishment, many consumers feel it's their right or obligation to file for damages—even when they spill it on themselves.

The industry wants to create and sell enjoyable hot drinks, but how integral is high temperature to the flavor and customers' enjoyment of coffee? The reality is that it's a crucial element. Industry studies demonstrate that high brewing temperatures create optimal flavor in coffee, and consumers concur, emphasizing consistently that they prefer their coffee hot—not warm. However, the optimal range of brewing temperatures—the very same factor that renders coffee flavorful— also turns a customer's occasional spill into a burn risk and lawsuit.

Today's coffee retail environment is crowded with opportunities for sales in almost any venue: traditional coffee shops, fast food outlets, convenience stores, supermarkets, kiosks, carts, stadiums, airport and train terminals, etc.. We are a mobile culture and have "to-go" expectations. We drink beverages while we drive. We've installed cup holders in cars, trucks, snowmobiles, and even motorcycles. We've created drive-through lanes and have stressed the convenience and speed of delivery from establishment to vehicle. We've increased the size and portability of most food products we consume. We want and make it increasingly easier to multi-task. Now we've added cell phones and other mobile devices into the mix—talking and texting, watching the GPS, checking the internet—all while driving two tons of steel with one hand on the wheel, one hand holding a beverage or phone, and one eye on the road. We're running out of hands and eyes!

In the midst of this hectic, demanding, consumer-driven retail environment, the hot beverage industry weighs its consumers' product expectations and preferences with the product's hazard risks. This is a challenging equation to balance, particularly when you consider that the temperatures involved in creating and maintaining a quality product usually pose little or no risk when consumed as intended; yet, when the product is mishandled, spilled, jostled, or dropped, it can pose serious burn risks.

Unfortunately, consumer-spilled hot coffee litigation cases continue with no end in sight. In terms of costs, a company can spend only so much on such customer claims before it feels an obligation to fight back. The image of the business and future sales are at risk; companies cannot afford to ignore public perception of misconduct.

In order to protect consumers, food and beverage safety standards have been primarily concerned with the microbiological hazards of food safety and the sanitation of handler environments. Restaurant restrooms have mandatory signs requiring employees to wash their hands properly before handling food or serving customers. Many restaurants, following Food and Drug Administration (FDA) guidelines, have placed a warning statement in small print at the bottom of their menus, such as "consuming raw or undercooked meats, poultry, seafood, shellfish, or eggs may increase your risk of food borne illness."

Now another food and beverage safety concern is open for interpretation and litigation: the temperature of the beverage. What are the solutions to this problem? First, retailers must create an internal culture of safety; it is essential that pertinent technical awareness be taught and implemented. Secondly, the coffee, tea, and hot cocoa industries must join ranks to educate the public about why these minimum temperature standards are necessary in terms of flavor, as well as to raise awareness about the degree of caution required in handling hot beverages safely.

When people burn themselves, it is not frivolous. Although it can be a serious incident, sometimes it also can be a frivolous lawsuit. There is an important line between what is generally accepted as a reasonable risk in consuming a hot product and what is truly dangerous. For the hot beverage industry, the Liebeck case illustrated the importance of approaching burn incidents from a beverage quality and a legal perspective. In that particular case, McDonald's was within industry standards for temperature; however, their handling of the incident was seen as callous and unsympathetic. McDonald's lacked proper and authoritative validation of industry brewing and holding standards, and it lacked useful warning descriptions for consumers that clarified why certain temperatures are necessary for quality.

For judges and juries, the technical issues surrounding the necessity of high temperatures in order to achieve consumer acceptable taste requirements need to be understood; for plaintiffs, the incentive to obtain huge awards in frivolous lawsuits should become dubious, at best; and for defense teams, successfully shielding the industry from frivolous litigation should become paramount.

CHAPTER 1

Industry Standards: Brewing, Holding, and Serving Hot Beverages

Coffee: Creating an Enjoyable Beverage

The hot beverage industry strives to produce quality beverages that consumers enjoy and producing an enjoyable cup of coffee means brewing and holding the beverage properly. The temperatures used for brewing are above the skin burn threshold and are important to the brewing process; they also are a large piece of the hot beverage litigation puzzle.

The premise of brewing coffee—technically, extraction—is to take ground coffee, a solid, and combine it with hot water to turn it into a consumable liquid. The brewing process utilizes hot water for a specific amount of time to extract the proper amount of soluble solids and other flavor compounds from the ground coffee. Three paramount variables here are (1) the water-to-grounds ratio, called the throw weight, (2) the temperature of the water, and (3) the time required to complete the proper extraction. Although the process seems simple, many variables must be managed well in order to achieve an enjoyable cup of coffee. Three primary variables are described as follows: Product, Process, and People.

The Product

Prior to brewing, coffee beans are a neutral agricultural product. Coffee becomes valuable when processed into a drinkable beverage for consumption. Brewed coffee consists of approximately 98% water; it is essentially flavored water.

If the product does not taste good—fails in the cup—it is usually due to natural attributes (faults and taints) that make it taste undesirable, or it is either over-roasted and burnt, under-roasted and sour. The working definition for taints is: undesirable sensory attributes resulting in unexpected flavors or aromas, which cause the coffee to be unsound, but not necessarily rejected by the consumer. Faults are defined primarily as cup defects that impart flavor or aroma that distract from the coffee's character and cause unsoundness and thus rejection of the coffee.

The quality of water used for extraction cannot be understated, and industry standards reflect that need. If tainted water is used, then the product will be impaired. Furthermore, coffee may be too weakly or strongly brewed, or it may be thin and watery due to a low brew temperature. Consumers rarely file litigation over the taste of coffee: they ask either for a new cup or for their money returned. Sometimes an unsatisfactory beverage will mean a loss of customer loyalty, but likely not a lawsuit.

There is a perception that chemical fertilizers, pesticides, and herbicides (all of which may be used in the process of growing coffee) are inherently harmful to consumers. The process of roasting coffee in temperatures above 400°F virtually eliminates these potential dangers by roasting away the compounds. Only a miniscule trace amount—on the order of parts per billion or trillion—of those compounds may remain.

The Process

During the brewing process, extracting the proper amounts of solids and other flavor compounds from the coffee grounds creates an enjoyable cup. The key element in this extraction process is hot water. The industry wide temperature recommendation for proper extraction is 195° to 205°F. Extensive studies confirm that these temperatures create the proper beverage.[2,3] The use of lower temperature creates a thin, under-extracted cup, and higher water temperature creates an astringent, bitter or sour, over-extracted cup. Because of the impact of water temperature on beverage quality, this brewing temperature range has become an industry standard for both commercial and consumer brewers. The infusion (contact) time is also important. A brewing process that takes too long or is too quick will result in an undesirable cup. Brewer manufacturers understand this necessity and the new generation of coffee brewers come equipped with built-in timers, high and low temperature sensors, as well as tamper-proof features. This assures consistency of the finished product as well as some safety features for the user.

The People

Another significant variable in the process of delivering a good cup of coffee is the server and his or her interaction with the customers. People are the most error-prone variable in the process.

Servers can account for error in any phase of the brewing process—from bean-to-cup. In addition to the brewing process, customers often communicate their orders to servers in hectic, noisy environments, or through drive-thru speakers and orders may be complex or differ from the terminology that servers use. Each person has his or her own specific preferences and expectations when it comes to coffee: a taste, temperature, or condiment preferred by one might be intolerable to another. For these reasons and many more, a server might present the wrong coffee order to the consumer. Training serving staff is expensive and employee turnover seems constant; thus, the serving responsibility frequently falls into the hands of the least experienced employee and makes an already tricky situation trickier.

Conclusion

The Product, Process, and People involved in serving a good cup of coffee or other hot beverage successfully come together countless times every day. However, it is necessary to also concern ourselves with the handful of times and unfortunate cases when a variable can be a factor in a burn-inducing spill. Human error as well as defective ancillary products such as cups, lids, to-go mugs, and carrying trays, all provide opportunities for consumers to spill coffee on themselves and potentially take the retailer to court. The training, knowledge, skill of the servers, as well as the quality and ease of use of supplemental coffee products must always be at the forefront of the retailer's concern for consumer safety when serving hot beverages.

Brewing, Holding, and Serving Coffee

Temperature is important in three distinct periods in the life of the coffee beverage: brewing, holding, and serving. The brewing and holding temperature of the coffee impact the beverage physically and chemically, and thus affect the beverage's flavor profile and aroma when served. All grades of coffee—commercial, premium, and specialty—are affected by the temperature of brewing and holding conditions.

Brewing Conditions: Temperature

In the United States, the filter drip method is the most popular way of brewing coffee, whether preparation happens at home or in retail establishments. As a result, the design of coffee makers has evolved to become more efficient, precise, and easier to use.

Only two ingredients are required to make drip coffee: coffee and hot water. To make the coffee beans into a beverage, the green coffee beans are roasted, ground, and then infused with hot water. The process of infusing ground coffee with water is referred to as brewing or extracting. Typically, the coffee is ground so that water can reach more of the beans' surface area and the brewing process can extract the correct amount of the beans' solids and other compounds.

The variables involved in the brewing process include water temperature (brew temperature), how finely or coarsely ground the coffee beans are (grind size), the ratio of coffee to water (throw weight), and the brew cycle (infusion) time. The grind size is impossible to change after the coffee has been brewed, and the strength of the coffee is not typically altered except by human intervention (via the addition of creamer, for example). The manufacturer of the coffee brewing machine usually sets brew cycle time. However, the temperature of the water, and subsequently the coffee beverage, can be highly variable and change between brewing and drinking time.

The person making the coffee or the machine regulates brewing temperature. There are seven main methods of brewing coffee: direct infusion (pouring water over the coffee grounds without a filter), percolation, filter drip coffee, vacuum system brewer, French press/plunger pot, single-cup brewers, espresso, and instant coffee (soluble). Filter drip coffee refers to both a drip system where water is poured manually over coffee grounds and through a filter, and an automated drip coffee brewing machine that regulates the temperature and flow of water over the grounds.

Company	Brew Volume	Temp. Range	Factory Set Temp.
FETCO	single 1gal to twin 2gal single and twin 3gal 6-24 gallon capacity	180-208°F	**Tank: 205°F; spray head 195±5**
Curtis	72oz 60oz 1.5gallons 3gal/6gal/10gal 1gal/1.5gal	170-204°F	**200°F**
BUNN	most BUNN brewers	—	**200°F**

Today, the automated drip machine is the most common type of commercial coffee brewing machine in use in the US. Automated drip coffee brewers are also built for home use. Industry regulations for commercial coffee brewers dictate brewing temperature of 195°F-205°F. Most manufacturers set machines to a default temperature setting, but also have a range of temperatures available if the owner of

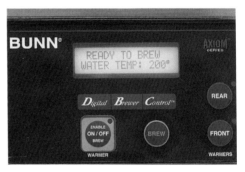

Example of standard factory set temperature setting.

the machine prefers a different temperature. Most, if not all, manufacturers have high-limit thermostats that shut off the heat source if the water temperature goes above 205°F.

The 195°F to 205°F brewing temperature range was established by the Coffee Brewing Center of the Pan-American Coffee Bureau through the research of Dr. Earl Lockhart in 1952.[1] During sensory analyses, the coffee was determined to have the most pleasing balance of acidity, body, bitterness, and astringency in this temperature range. All four components of coffee flavor increased in intensity with an increase in the brew temperature.[2] Although acidity and body are considered desirable traits, bitterness and astringency are not. It is advantageous to have a coffee product with the greatest flavor and with the least amount of undesirable flavor traits. The range of 195°F to 205°F for brew temperature was determined in sensory analyses to satisfy a balancing act between the intensity of the acidity and body and the intensity of the bitterness and astringency. Temperatures higher than 205°F resulted in an undesirable coffee flavor and temperatures lower than 195°F resulted in poor extraction from the coffee grounds, which diminished the aroma and flavor of the beverage.

Chemical analyses of coffee brewed at different temperatures confirm the sensory findings: there are significant differences in the chemical composition of coffee brewed at different temperatures.[2] Therefore, as a general principle, the higher the brew temperature the greater the extraction of all types of chemical compounds from the coffee bean. The amount of chemical compounds extracted from the coffee beans has a direct influence on the intensity of the flavor profile (acidity, body, bitterness, astringency). Chemical analyses show that the 195°F to 205°F range of brew temperature causes the proper extraction rate of chemical compounds from the coffee and makes coffee with the best flavor profile.[2]

Holding Conditions: Holding Vessels, Temperature, and Time

For the flavor of brewed coffee to remain optimal, three factors are involved: (1) how the coffee is held, (2) at what temperature the coffee is held, and (3) how long the coffee is held.

Two ways of storing brewed coffee are in an open decanter (pot or carafe), or in a closed container (an urn or airpot). The decanter is usually kept on a hot plate and is therefore exposed to a constant temperature of approximately 185°F (as measured from the middle of a decanter on a BUNN hot plate after fifteen minutes). Urns range from 1.5 to 10 gallons in size, whereas airpots usually contain 2 liters of liquid. Both urns and airpots provide insulation for the coffee but do not directly heat it. The length of time coffee is held in these containers is variable from business to business, and often depends on frequency of use and time of day. Industry standards dictate holding temperatures are ideal between 175°F and 185°F. It is also important to maintain a constant holding temperature within this range: the Coffee Brewing Center has stated, "any fluctuation of temperature will cause the flavor to break down more rapidly." [3]

These three factors (holding vessel, temperature, and time) ideally combine into a stable environment to best preserve coffee's volatile aromatic and fragile taste compounds.[2] To maintain coffee's delicate flavor profile, the manner in which the coffee is held must control for three things.

1. **The rate at which the aromatic compounds are driven out of the brew.**

    Aromatic compounds equate with the smell of the brewed coffee beverage. The more these compounds evaporate out of the coffee, the less the coffee is going to give off the typical pleasant coffee aroma.

    The aromatic coffee compounds are almost all compounds that have reached their boiling point (which are all below the boiling point of water). Once reaching their boiling point, they are in a gaseous state and leave the surface of the coffee as soon as the coffee is exposed to air. As the gases leave the coffee, the aromatics of the coffee change and lessen. The decrease in the aromatics is a function of how the coffee is held.

    If the coffee is housed in a closed container, the gases leave the coffee until the vapor pressure in the container reaches equilibrium, at which point the gases leave and enter the coffee at the same rate.[2] By keeping coffee in a sealed container, the gases reach equilibrium between the coffee and the top of the container, and the aromatics are mostly preserved.

2. **The rate at which the taste compounds change within the coffee.**

    The compounds that make up the taste of the coffee beverage that have not reached their boiling point play a role in the taste of the coffee. The rate at which the taste compounds change is a function primarily of the holding temperature, how that temperature is maintained, and length of hold time.

    Chlorogenic acid, at approximately 15% of the soluble compounds in brewed coffee, has the most impact on the coffee's taste. When chlorogenic acid breaks down, it breaks down into caffeic and quinic acids. The higher the level of these acids, the more sour and bitter the coffee becomes. Therefore, it is desirable to hold coffee at temperatures in which chlorogenic acid is most stable. It is important to hold coffee at a temperature in which chlorogenic acid remains stable because this acid makes up a large amount of the soluble concentration in the finished brew.[2]

    Studies done at the Coffee Brewing Center have shown that chlorogenic acid is most stable between 175°F and 185°F. Applied heat and prolonged exposure to heat (as in the case of a decanter of coffee being left on a burner), increases the chemical changes taking place in the beverage. Therefore, insulated containers, such as airpots, are best for slowing the breakdown of chlorogenic acid and other compounds in the coffee.

    Coffee industry standards dictate holding coffee at temperatures between 175°F and 185°F and recommend that coffee be held in insulated containers away from direct heat.

3. **The rate at which water evaporates from the coffee**

    Brewed coffee is 98.65% to 98.85% water and only 1.15% to 1.35% soluble material.[3] The ratio of water to coffee is important when brewing and it is also significant when holding the coffee after brewing. The rate of evaporation is a function of liquid and air temperature, and air-exposed surface area.

    The more water that evaporates, the greater the concentration of soluble materials in the beverage—the coffee becomes stronger and more potent. The breakdown of chlorogenic acid and other soluble materials in combination with the increased concentration of these compounds due to water evaporation creates a highly unpleasant taste.[3]

    To avoid water evaporation from the coffee while maintaining its temperature at 175°F-185°F, it is advisable to keep the coffee in a sealed, insulated container.

Holding time is one of the most variable elements of served coffee. As with many businesses, coffee retailers experience lulls and rushes of customers and during some parts of the day those times are predictable. Even so, it is still hard to predict accurately how much coffee to brew at any given time of day. A customer could walk in the door right after the coffee has been brewed or when an airpot or decanter of coffee has been sitting for an hour or more. Some coffee businesses have set a certain time limit after which they throw the coffee away and brew a fresh pot. This helps regulate how long coffee sits before reaching the consumer, although a lot of coffee can be wasted.

Even if held at 175°F-185°F, the flavor of the coffee will still break down over time. The Coffee Brewing Center concluded that a hold time of one hour was acceptable as there was no noticeable loss of flavor within that timeframe. However, after one hour the coffee flavor worsened rapidly.[3] If coffee is held in an open decanter on a warmer, it is recommended that it only be held for 20 minutes.[2]

In summary, to maintain brewed coffee at optimal freshness, it is necessary to hold the coffee in a sealed, insulated container at 175°F-185°F, and only allow an hour or less to pass between brewing and serving.

Serving Conditions: Temperature and Serving Vessels

Temperature

When a customer is served a cup of coffee, four senses are involved—sight, touch, smell, and taste. Assuming the coffee was brewed properly to attain the best level of extraction from the grounds, and assuming the coffee was held to maintain the freshness of the beverage as much as possible, then the beverage possesses optimal aromatics, flavor, and color at presentation to the customer. How the customer sees and feels the beverage is then determined by how the coffee is delivered and served.

If the customer is presented the cup of coffee without a lid, they can see its color and an indication of the temperature because of evaporation rising from the cup *(see Appendix)*. They then experience the coffee tactilely when

Examples of Airpots

grasping the cup and likely feel the heat of the beverage through the cup's walls. With the first sips, he or she can smell the coffee, feel its heat and mouth-feel, as well as taste the beverage.

Depending on the type of cup used, the color of the beverage is either displayed or masked. When coffee is served lidded or in a to-go mug, the customer is not able to judge the color of the coffee or its temperature (without seeing evaporation).

The feel of the beverage (namely its temperature) can be determined by grasping the cup and feeling the heat through the cup (although a handle on a ceramic cup, etc., might bypass this tactile judgment). The feel of the beverage also occurs when the customer comes into direct contact with the beverage during sipping or drinking.

Although brewing and holding temperatures are very important to coffee's aromatics and flavor profiles, the serving temperature is equally important in terms of the burn risk. Serving temperature is the temperature at which the customer first contacts the beverage. It is the one aspect that most greatly influences the experience of drinking coffee (sight, smell, taste, and feel) and that can be adjusted at the time of service.

The smell and taste of coffee has been shown to be optimal at holding temperatures of 175°F-185°F.[2] Held at too low a temperature the coffee loses its aromatics and its flavor profile changes.[2] The experience of coffee through smell and taste over time demonstrates that coffee loses its sensory appeal at holding temperatures that are too low. This sets a lower limit, so to speak, on holding and serving temperatures of coffee.

The tactile experience of coffee within the mouth reveals that there are temperatures at which coffee is painful and potentially can be damaging to the mouth tissues. In other words, there are temperatures at which coffee is too hot for consumption without pain or risk of burning. This sets an upper limit on the serving temperatures of coffee. The sensory experience of coffee is therefore a balancing act between the lower limits of enjoyable taste and smell and the upper limits of the mouth's pain threshold.

Just as taste preferences and pain thresholds vary from person to person, lower limit and upper limit temperature preferences differ as well. Some people might prefer to drink coffee at their upper temperature limit, close to brew temperature (these people are jokingly said to have "asbestos mouth"). Other people do not. Although brewing and holding standard temperatures have been set from professional sensory and chemical analyses, serving temperature generally is a matter of consumers' personal preferences and expectations regarding how hot coffee is "meant to be" served.

Table 1: Temperatures used in O'Mahony temperature preference research
Mean temperatures of coffees immediately after dispensing in the cup[4]

102.5 °F	A temperature below reported pain thresholds in the oral cavity
121.6 °F	A temperature inflicting pain but likely to be below the damage for coffee kept in the mouth for only a few (approx 5) seconds
141.7 °F	A temperature slightly above the threshold for epidermal damage for a hot stimulus of a few seconds duration
161.8 °F	Normal serving temperature
169.8 °F	Normal serving temperature
179.8 °F	Normal serving temperature

Personal Preferences of Serving Temperature: the O'Mahony Studies

To determine appropriate ranges for serving temperatures, the Coffee Quality Institute (CQI) contacted Professor M. O'Mahony of the University of California Davis in 1998 about this gap in knowledge. O'Mahony conducted a number of experiments funded by a grant from the Folgers Coffee Company and donations of time and equipment by the Specialty Coffee Association of America and BUNN-O-Matic. These experiments studied the temperature at which people prefer to consume coffee.[4,5,6] In addition, O'Mahony conducted other studies concerning temperature preferences for both black coffee versus coffee with creamer and stronger versus weaker coffee. Another segment of experiments produced observational data on when people took their first sip of coffee and measured the temperature of the first sip.

In one experiment, he gave participants six different temperatures of black coffee to rank from most preferred to least preferred temperature. In this paradigm, the most preferred temperature was 161.8°F (approximately 75% of participants "liked" this temperature). To test temperature preference in a different paradigm, he conducted an experiment where he gave participants pots of hotter and colder coffee and instructed them to mix the two until they arrived at their most preferred temperature. The average preferred temperature in this paradigm was 139.6°F.[4]

Perhaps surprisingly, the two most preferred temperatures had a discrepancy of 22.2°F. A number of factors in O'Mahony's two experiments point to why there was such a difference. In the first experiment, participants were instructed to take a small amount of coffee (less than 30mL) and sip it. In the second study, participants were instructed to drink the coffee. The process of sipping could have cooled the temperature of the coffee, and the temperature in the mouth of the participant could have been less than the temperature measured right before consumption. Thus, sipping the coffee in the first experiment most likely cooled the most preferred temperature of the first experiment (161.8°F) to a temperature closer to the average most preferred temperature of the second experiment (139.6°F) during which the coffee was drunk and not sipped.

To explore further the discrepancy between the first and second experiment, O'Mahony collected data from 33 participants who agreed to perform the second experiment (the mixing paradigm) 10 times on different days. The temperature each consumer chose as preferred during the different sessions varied considerably. The mean range of variation for each consumer across the 10 sessions was 21.6°F.[4] The difference between the first experiment's most preferred temperature and the second experiment's average preferred temperature was 22.2°F. The preferred consumption temperature across 10 different experimental sessions (22.2°F) varied about the same amount as the difference between the first and second experiment's most preferred temperature (21.6°F). Thus, the discrepancy between the experiments (161.8°F vs. 139.6°F) can also be attributed to normal consumer preference variation.

O'Mahony also collected observational data in coffee shops around the UC Davis campus to determine when consumers took their first sip or drink of coffee. He measured the temperatures of cups of coffee to get data on the typical cooling curves of served coffee. He then applied those temperature curves to the observational data of the time elapsed until first sip to determine the average temperature at which consumers took their first sip or drink of coffee.

Approximately 75% of both black and creamed coffee consumers took their first sip within three minutes of service. For black coffee drinkers, the most common time interval between service and first sip or drink was 30-60 seconds. For creamed coffee drinkers, the most common time interval was 60-90 seconds. Applying temperature curves, the mean temperature at first sip (for black coffee drinkers) was 168°F.[4] Coffee with cream or sugar added would be at variable temperature and therefore O'Mahony was unable to apply his temperature curves to creamed or sugared coffee. It can be assumed that coffee with cream or sugar added would be cooler due to the addition and the possible agitation and/or stirring needed to mix the beverage.

"Comparing these real temperature data for drinking with the preferred and liked temperatures, it would seem that most of the customers were taking their first sip at temperatures above those which they would prefer," O'Mahony observed.[4] O'Mahony went on to discuss two possibilities for this discrepancy in his report. The first possibility is degree of error in estimation of first sip temperatures, and the second is that the consumers used the first sip to make a judg-

Table 2: Ranking Paradigm: Drinking Temperature Preferences
Preference for temperatures at which to drink black coffee[4]

Temperature	Percentage of judges who liked this temperature
161.8 °F *Most Preferred*	74.2%
141.7 °F	63.6%
169.8 °F	40.9%
121.6 °F	16.4%
179.8 °F	9.8%
102.5 °F *Least Preferred*	3.1%

Table 3: Ranking Paradigm: Expected Serving Temperatures
Order of temperatures that judges thought would most likely be found for
black coffee served in coffee shop[4]

Temperatures	Percentage of judges who would not be surprised at having coffee served at this temperature
167.2 °F *Most Expected*	99.1%
144.7 °F	93.0%
177.2 °F	80.3%
186.3 °F	59.6%
123.5 °F	23.9%
103.7 °F *Least Expected*	5.2%

ment of the temperature of the coffee and subsequently waited longer to drink at a more preferable temperature. O'Mahony refers to this initial sip as an exploratory sip.

O'Mahony pointed out that there was substantial variation in the temperature of the coffee when it was served and that consumer behavior with the coffee after it was served was also variable. Some customers would stir and/or agitate their coffee, which could contribute to heat loss[4]. If an error of ±10°F was considered, this would reduce the discrepancy between the estimated temperature at first sip (168°F) and the preferred temperatures from the two experiments (161.8°F and 139.6°F). It is also valuable to consider that most regular coffee drinkers have a ritual of drinking their coffee. This ritual can have major impacts on the temperature of the beverage they consume, depending on how they prepare their beverage and whether they add cream/sugar, how long they wait to take their first sip of coffee, how long they wait to actually drink their coffee, and the amount of time they take to finish the coffee. These variations were not accounted for in O'Mahony's temperature curves.

The second possible reason for the discrepancy can be found in discussing the function of the first sip of coffee. O'Mahony postulated, "the first sip could well have been an exploratory sip." Assuming the consumer is unable to fully judge the temperature of the coffee from visual and tactile cues, it makes sense that the first sip of coffee is the consumer's most reliable way of determining the temperature of the beverage and whether that is his or her preferred drinking temperature. *(Table 2)*

Expectations of Serving Temperature

O'Mahony also addressed the consumer's expectations of serving temperatures. In O'Mahony's ranking paradigm, he asked participants to rank six different temperatures of coffee from preferred to least preferred. After they ranked their preferences, he asked them to rank their serving temperature expectations, from most to least expected. The expectations ranking was obtained by the consumer first pouring "a full cup of coffee from each server into a paper cup and immediately [judging] the temperature…Some consumers judged coffee temperature by feeling the cup with their hands and did not drink the coffee, some judged just by sipping and swallowing the coffee, while others judged by doing both."[4]

For each of the six temperatures, participants were asked which temperatures would not surprise them if they were served in coffee shops *(Table 3)*. The most expected temperature was 167.2°F (99% of participants would not be surprised to be served this temperature). The second and third most expected temperatures were 144.7°F (~93% would not be surprised to be served this temperature) and 177.2°F (~80% would not be surprised to be served this temperature) respectively *(see Tables 2 and 3)*.[4]

It is important to note that O'Mahony accounted for temperature loss caused

Table 4: Coffee brewing, holding, and serving temperature loss over time

		Temperature	Temperature loss due to...
C O O L I N G	**AUTOMATED DRIP COFFEE BREWING MACHINE**	195-205°F	
	↓		
	Water exits machine, hitting ground coffee		Water passing through grounds, time
	↓		
	Water passes through the grounds		
	↓		
	Coffee exits the brew basket		
	Coffee enters the airpot		
	↓		
	AIRPOT	175-185°F	
	Coffee sits in airpot		Transfer from airpot to cup
	↓		
	Coffee is pumped from airpot		
	Coffee enters cup	165-175°F	Material of cup
	↓		
	CUP		
	If creamer is added...	decreases ~4°F[2]	
	↓		
	First sip	168°F[4]	
	↓		
	Drinking the coffee	140°F[4]	

by pouring the coffee in small amounts (approximately 30 mL). He therefore had two different temperature categories: temperatures measured from a full cup of coffee (used to rank expected serving temperatures) and temperatures measured in the amount that the participants would have consumed when ranking their preference for serving temperatures. Although these temperatures were different, they represented different points on a cooling curve after starting at an original base temperature. Therefore, the author refers to these temperatures with the same origin as temperature sets.

The top three preferred temperatures and the top three expected serving temperatures are the same temperature sets. It is interesting to note the consistency between preferred and expected serving temperatures. Extensive chemical and sensory data were not always available to explain which temperatures should be used to brew, hold, and serve coffee, and coffee has been successfully served hot for hundreds of years. Significant precedence has been set for the average consumer to assume they will receive a reasonably hot beverage when ordering coffee. The relationship between personal preference and expectations is a rather murky issue. Which influences which? Does our expectation that coffee ought to be hot determine what we prefer to drink, or does what we prefer to drink determine what we expect to be served? Personal preference and expectation of coffee temperatures will most likely remain entwined.

In summary of the O'Mahony studies, the mean most preferred coffee temperature was found to be 139.6°F (mixing paradigm) and the most preferred temperature was found to be 161.8°F (ranking paradigm). The average variation by the same participant over 10 repetitions of the mixing paradigm was 21.6°F, which can account for the 22.2°F difference in preferred temperatures (other differences between the paradigms such as drinking versus sipping can also account for the discrepancy). The most expected serving temperature was found to be 167.2°F (same temperature set as the most preferred temperature).

Considering these data, serving temperatures should be no lower than 140°F and no higher than 175°F. Because the coffee cools when it is poured from holding container to serving container, and because coffee cools as it is being drunk, it is advantageous to serve coffee in the upper portion of the recommended range. It is impractical to serve coffee that is too cold to be pleasing to a range of consumers, and to have to expend more time and energy to reheat the beverage. O'Mahony observes: "The fact that customers did not always rush to drink their coffee immediately after pouring would suggest that they had learned by experience that a waiting period was necessary [to cool the coffee to the preferred temperature]."[4] Thus, coffee served between 165°F-175°F (the most expected serving temperature being 167.2°F) will satisfy the majority of consumers: those who prefer their coffee to be hotter will be satisfied, and those who prefer their coffee cooler will wait for the coffee to cool to the preferred temperature.

Vessels: To-Go Cups, Lids, Sleeves, and Carriers

The cooling curves of a hot beverage after it is served are somewhat dependent on the type of cup used for serving, the volume of the beverage (size of the cup), and how much of the beverage is exposed to the air (whether it is lidded or not).

Common serving sizes for to-go cups are 8 oz., 12 oz., 16 oz., 20 oz., and 24 oz., with some smaller or larger cup variations at certain locations. Most to-go cups in the US do not have handles. The most variable aspect of cup design is the material of which cups are made. Common materials are polystyrene, ceramic, and paper. Polystyrene cups are slightly more insulating than paper cups, and therefore, they keep the beverage hotter longer and are not as hot to the touch. Potentially, this discourages double-cupping because the cup is easier to handle, however, it could mislead the customer into thinking the beverage is not as hot as it actually is.

Double-cupping is a term employed when two to-go cups are stacked one inside the other to provide more heat protection than a sleeve. Double-cupping is usually provided only upon request as most retailers prefer customers to use a cheaper and less wasteful sleeve. It is unknown whether the act of double-cupping adds to or impinges upon the structural integrity of the cup. It is also unclear if double-cupping could cause a problem with the seal of the lid or contribute to lid malfunctions.

Lids are usually designed to fit more than one size of cup. However, it is common to see at least two lid sizes to go with the range of cup sizes offered.

Sleeves can be put on cups (usually on paper cups, which are harder to handle if the coffee is hot). These cut down on the number of requests for drinks to be double-cupped. Sleeves usually fit the medium to larger sized cups, but can be too big to accommodate the smaller sized cups (such as 8 oz.).

Beverage carriers are also available to help customers carry multiple drinks. These carriers are usually designed to fit four cups and most cafés have these carriers. Some establishments make it policy to use them when a customer orders a certain number of drinks and some are provided only as needed or requested.

In the American to-go culture, hot beverages are consumed in cars, trucks, buses, airplanes, and other vehicles. Modern cars provide at least one cup holder and most likely several more, usually located between the driver's and passenger's seat, sometimes on the inside panel of driver and passenger doors, and occasionally in a backseat center console. In addition, many consumers walk while drinking or carrying coffee. These and other on-the-go opportunities to drink hot beverages provide many immensely satisfying coffee drinking moments, as well as many opportunities to spill and sue.

Espresso

An espresso beverage also involves coffee and water, but it is made in small quantities, quickly, and under pressure. The coffee that produces an espresso beverage is very finely ground and tamped into the brew basket of a portafilter that is then inserted into the espresso machine. Between one to three ounces of water is then forced through the coffee grounds using pressure and gravity.

Usually about 7 grams (g) of coffee and 30 milliliters (mL) of water are required to make one espresso beverage. Industry standards for espresso dictate that the water temperature be 190°F-200°F.[7] The 30 mL of water is forced through the coffee grounds at about 130 psi of pressure, for 25-30 seconds (although this varies by how finely or coarsely the coffee is ground).[1]

Espresso

Espresso is served as a single espresso, a double espresso, etc.. The term single typically refers to an espresso beverage of a little less than 30 mL, and the double, triple, etc. are multiples of that quantity.

Espresso, small in quantity and therefore fast cooling, is usually consumed relatively quickly after being served. In brief explorations at Coffee Enterprises, a single espresso lost, on average, 5°F a minute *(Table 6)*.

Espresso and steamed milk together in one beverage create another category of beverages that includes lattés and cappuccinos. In the case of lattés and cappuccinos, there is usually a greater quantity of steamed milk than espresso, so the temperature of the espresso does not have much of an effect on the temperature of the overall drink.

Steamed Milk Beverages

Steamed milk beverages encompass three different categories: steamed milk (called steamers), espresso and steamed milk beverages (lattés and cappuccinos). The process of steaming milk can also be called foaming or frothing the milk.

Steamed Milk

Steaming, frothing, or foaming milk is the process of heating milk with steam.[8] Milk is usually kept refrigerated at around 40°F. A quantity of milk is poured into a pitcher, and a steam wand (usually incorporated in an espresso machine) is put about an inch below the surface of the milk. The wand is turned on and produces steam at 230°F at pressure. The steam jet usually causes the milk to spin. It heats and air is drawn into the milk as it steams. The air that is drawn into the milk attaches to some of the milk's proteins, which causes the milk to increase in volume. The two most important changes due to the process of steaming milk are an increase in temperature and an increase in volume.

The temperature of the milk as it is steamed is controlled either by a machine or by the person steaming the milk. Industry standards for temperature-sensitive steam wands dictate an upper limit temperature of approximately 158°F when the steam wand shuts off.[9] If the machine does not possess a temperature-sensitive steam wand, it is necessary for the person steaming the milk to use a thermometer to monitor the temperature of the milk. The temperature of steamed milk should be between 150° and 160°F.[8] Milk will begin to exhibit a scalded or burnt flavor if heated above 170°F. This effect is due to the whey proteins in the milk cooking and producing an aroma and flavor that is undesirable to a large majority of consumers.[6] Unlike the O'Mahony studies for coffee, temperature preference studies for steamed milk beverages have not been done extensively. However, the range of 150°F-160°F is widely found throughout espresso literature as the recommendation for steamed milk temperatures.

The industry recommendations for steamed milk temperature are thus 150°F-160°F.[8] As with drip coffee, a steamed milk drink loses temperature continually from the moment it is made, poured into a cup, and served. The temperature at which it reaches a consumer is lower than the temperature to which it was originally steamed. In brief experiments done at Coffee Enterprises, it was found that a steamed milk beverage lost approximately 2°F per minute, even with different pour rates or with simulated drinking and subsequent volume loss (*see Table 5*).

Unpublished Trials/Experiments Done at Coffee Enterprises

Table 5: Temperature loss of steamed milk in a 12 oz. paper cup with simulated sipping

Time Elapsed	Temperature
When it stopped steaming	153.3 °F
1min	150.8 °F
2min	149.0 °F
3min	146.7 °F
4min	144.4 °F
5min	142.6 °F
6min	140.9 °F
7min	139.4 °F
8min	137.8 °F
9min	135.6 °F
10min	133.5 °F

Average temperature loss while "sipping" = 2 °F

Table 6: Temperature loss of a single shot of espresso

Time Elapsed	Temperature
Immediately	165.2 °F
1min	154.4 °F
2min	149.7 °F
3min	146.0 °F
4min	142.3 °F
5min	139.0 °F

Average temperature loss per minute = 5 °F

Table 7: Temperature loss over three hours in an airpot of coffee

Brand & Size	Curtis Large
Coffee/Water	9oz coffee/1.5gal water
Brew Time	6:40 min
Time Elapsed	Temperature
0 minutes	183.1 °F
30 minutes	180.3 °F
1 hour	179.0 °F
1.5 hours	178.1 °F
2 hours	177.0 °F
2.5 hours	176.0 °F
3 hours	175.1 °F

Average temperature loss every 30 minutes in airpot = 1.3 °F

Lattés and Cappuccinos

As described earlier, espresso is typically mixed with steamed milk to create drinks such as lattés and cappuccinos. The espresso is usually mixed with a greater quantity of steamed milk. When the two are mixed together, the steamed milk dominates the temperature of the drink because of its greater volume. The temperature of lattés and cappuccinos are therefore very similar to the temperature of steamed milk, however slightly more heat loss might occur due to a slightly longer period of preparation.

Cappuccino

Tea

Making hot tea beverages involves tea and hot water, and the brewing or steeping process involves an infusion of hot water usually brought to a boil right before infusion (thus at a temperature a little less than 212°F). Water must be at least 195°F for most teas.[10] However, certain teas are sometimes prepared at temperatures as low as 140°F and 160°F.[10] The tea is either contained in a tea bag or is loose leaf tea. The steeping process lasts anywhere from two to five minutes depending on the type of tea involved.[11]

Unlike coffee, tea is commonly prepared by the cup or by the pot in a commercial setting, and there is little if any hold time of the infused beverage. A small percentage of Americans are hot tea drinkers, which is why many teas are made to order instead of kept in urns or airpots.

The two temperatures of concern with tea are steeping and serving temperatures. Tea is prepared for a customer by boiling water in a teakettle, or by drawing water from a hot water dispenser or spigot of a commercial coffee brewer. Many coffee and tea retailers prefer to use the hot water dispensed from their coffee brewer because it saves counter space and is a faster process than boiling water. Most commercial hot water dispensers have default temperature settings at 201°F, 202°F, or 205°F, depending on the size of the dispenser and its specific function[12]. Water drawn from the spigot of a coffee brewer is typically drawn from the same reservoir of water used to make coffee. Thus, water drawn from the hot water spigot of a coffee brewer is going to be between 195°F-205°F (FETCO default temperatures are set at 205°F, while Curtis and BUNN default temperatures are set at 200°F).[12, 13, 14]

If a customer orders tea to-go, it is usually prepared as fast as possible. Hot water (whether brought to a boil or poured from a spigot of a coffee brewer or other water heating device) is poured directly into the to-go cup and the tea is added before, during, or after the water is poured. The beverage is then delivered to the customer as soon as possible, and the customer is most likely instructed that steeping will take a few minutes.

Tea, therefore, is often available to be consumed immediately after and even during the steeping process. The typical serving temperature of tea is close to its steeping temperature because little time has passed between steeping and serving. There is usually little to no hold time and, therefore, minimal transfer into different containers that would contribute to heat loss. In brief trials done at Coffee Enterprises, a 20 oz. lidded paper cup of tea served at approximately 195°F lost an average of 1.6°F per minute in the first 10 minutes.

CHAPTER 2

Burns from Hot Beverages

Definition of a Burn

Technically, burns are "the degradation of the proteins in the epidermal tissue."[15] The function of a protein is dependent on its shape, and when exposed to extreme heat, proteins degrade or denature, losing their shape and thus their proper function.[16] A cell, dependent on the functions of its proteins, will die when its proteins are denatured.

Degrees of Burns

To understand burn degrees (the spectrum of burns possible), it is necessary to understand skin. The body's skin has two main layers. The epidermis is the thin top-most layer. The epidermis functions to waterproof the skin and is a barrier against infection. Underneath the epidermis is the dermis, which is thicker than the epidermis, cushions the body somewhat, and contains hair follicles, sweat glands, blood vessels, and other skin components. Below the dermis is a layer of tissue called the hypodermis that keeps the skin attached to the muscles and bones and other tissues that are below the skin.[16]

There are three general degrees of burns, all of which are possible to receive from hot liquid. Burns are classified by how deeply the damage extends into the skin. This depth of burn in turn influences the pain felt from the burn, the recovery time, and whether or not the burn leaves a scar.

First-degree burns damage part or all of the epidermis that contacts the burn medium. Second-degree burns damage all of the epidermis and extend into the dermis. First- and second-degree burns are referred to as partial thickness burns. Third degree burns damage the epidermis and all of the dermis and are therefore called full thickness burns *(see Table 8).*[7]

Types of Burns

There are five main types of burns: thermal, chemical, electrical, mechanical, and radiation. Burns resulting from a hot liquid fall into the thermal category. Thermal burns also include flame burns, contact burns from hot objects, explosion injuries, and sunburns.[17] A burn from a hot liquid is considered a scald contact burn.[18]

Burn Variables

Primary Variables: Temperature, Volume, Duration of Contact

The following three variables impact the burn severity of a scald contact burn most powerfully: the temperature and volume of the hot beverage, and the duration of contact with the burn medium. For example, if a person spills an entire 16 oz. cup of coffee (perhaps around 165°F) onto his lap while driving, the bev-

Table 8: Pain, burn depth, healing, and scarring associated with burn degrees[17]

Full/Partial Burn	Degree	Depth of Damage
Partial Thickness Burns	First Degree	Epidermis
Partial Thickness Burns	Second Degree *Superficial*	Epidermis and top of dermis
	Second Degree *Deep*	Epidermis and deep into dermis
Full Thickness Burns	Third Degree	Epidermis and all of dermis

erage will soak into his clothing and hold the heat close to his skin. In addition, he has to stop driving and remove the articles of clothing soaked in hot liquid before the contact with the heat is broken. Contrast this burn circumstance with a person who sloshes a quarter of her 16 oz. coffee (perhaps 4 oz. at 165°F) onto her arm when picking up the cup from the counter. The coffee will quickly roll off the skin, and even if it had soaked into a shirtsleeve, the shirt could be removed easily and quickly.

Third degree burns can be caused in one second of exposure to a 156°F liquid.[18] Thus the duration of contact in these two scenarios makes all the difference—the person in the car will most likely be exposed to the coffee spill for longer than a second as he tries to pull off the road, exit the car, and remove the soaked clothing. Even if the spill in the second scenario involved an entire 16 oz. cup of coffee on her hand and arm, this person would probably avoid third degree burn damage because the reaction to the burn would be quick and reflexive, and contact with the hot liquid would most likely last less than a second.

Secondary Variables

• *Burn Medium*

Volume of the liquid: The amount of liquid spilled that contacted the person.

Temperature of the liquid

Type of liquid: Different beverages could cause slightly different burn severity because of their different properties. A liquid with greater viscosity, such as syrup, would likely remain on the skin longer, thus potentially causing a more severe burn than would hot water at the same temperature and volume.

Pain	Heal Time	Scars?
Painful	5-7 days	No
Extreme pain and hypersensitivity	7-15 days	No
Usually painful	15-30 days	May leave hypertrophic/ thick scars
Usually not painful; nerve endings have been destroyed	REQUIRES SKIN GRAFTING	

- *Person Burned*

  Gender: Skin thicknesses and thus susceptibility to severe burns differ between genders. Men tend to have thicker skin than do women. A woman receiving a burn identical in all other aspects might suffer a slightly more severe burn.

  Age: Skin thickness and burn susceptibility differs in relation to age as well. Children and the elderly tend to have thinner skin than that of an adult and could therefore incur a slightly more severe burn.[19]

  Part of the Body: Skin thickness and burn susceptibility differ on different areas of the body. Burns in different parts of the body could also affect the level of pain experienced. For example, the palm of the hand has thick skin and requires higher temperature and/or longer exposure in order to burn in comparison to inner thigh skin, which is thinner.

- *Circumstance*

  Duration of exposure: How long the burn medium is in contact with the person's skin could vary due to circumstances in which the person cannot react reflexively and/or successfully avoid the burn medium.

  Medium of contact: Liquid has the ability to soak into other materials; therefore, a burn from a hot beverage could be acquired through a different medium than direct contact with the hot liquid. For example, if the hot liquid soaked into a person's clothing, it could hold the heat close to the person's skin longer and greatly change the reaction time of the person receiving the burn.

  Reaction time and reflexes: Under normal circumstances, a person who accidentally places his hand on a hot burner will almost immediately recoil and draw his hand away, breaking contact as soon as possible. This is an example of a withdrawal reflex. Withdrawal reflexes are measured in milliseconds.[20]

Spilling a hot liquid on oneself utilizes reflexes referred to above; however, the reflex might not necessarily be successful in avoiding harm. Depending on the volume and location of the spill on the body, and the circumstances of the spill, breaking contact with the burn medium could take much longer than the average reflexive reaction.

The Mouth vs. the Skin

Contact with a hot beverage falls into two realms: either it contacts the lips and mouth while it is drunk, or it is spilled on the person's skin. There are two main aspects that differ between drinking a hot beverage and contacting a hot beverage because of a spill: the amount of liquid and the body surfaces involved.

Amount of Liquid

The skin's surface area is very large in comparison to the surface area of mouth tissue. When drinking, people are only able to drink a certain amount of liquid at one time. When consuming a hot beverage, people tend to reduce the amount of liquid they consume at one time by sipping. Sipping is defined as consuming a very small amount of liquid: ~5 mL.[15] A spill usually involves much more liquid. The smaller the amount of hot liquid, the less heat energy it has; the less heat energy the liquid has, the less it will transfer heat to the surrounding tissues. Professor O'Mahony conducted a third study at U.C. Davis that recorded the temperature of coffee at various points within the cup and on the surface of a person's tongue. The study found that surface temperatures of the tongue were below the burn damage threshold after sipping and swallowing coffee at temperatures within the range of preferred drinking temperatures (140°F, 149°F, and 158°F).[6] At these temperatures, the sips of coffee were not in contact with the tongue surface long enough to raise the tongue tissue to a temperature that would result in burn damage.

Skin Surface

The O'Mahony data show that people are not only capable of ingesting liquid at temperatures between 140°F and 160°F, but moreover that they enjoy it; 140°F-160°F is the preferred range for consumption of coffee. The skin burn damage threshold (the temperature at which skin burns) is around 130°F.

To date, there have been very few studies regarding the impact of hot liquids on mouth tissues; therefore, not much is known about the burn threshold for pain and damage in the mouth.[15] However, the hot beverage industry can cite empirical and anecdotal data of the many thousands of years of experience in preparing and imbibing hot beverages that show overwhelming evidence that consumption of hot beverages is safe.[15]

It is worth mentioning here Fredericka Brown and Kenneth Diller's paper, "Calculating the Optimum Temperature for Serving Hot Beverages." Brown and Diller used the O'Mahony temperature preference data and combined this information with the skin damage risk of various temperatures of hot liquid. They recommended an "optimal drinking temperature of approximately 136°F," at which temperature they claim the risk of burn injury is minimized while consumer preference of temperature is maintained. They state: "The effect of the scald hazard is far more important at temperatures above the average consumer preferred drinking temperature than it is below. Clearly the combination of these two diverse considerations provides a rational basis for making a recommendation for hot beverage temperature." Brown and Diller also state "in all [of O'Mahony's] experiments the mean chosen drinking temperature for coffee was close to 60°C (140°F). This value is substantially lower than the industry recommended standards and would result in a substantial reduction in incidence and severity of scald injury in the event of a spill onto human skin."[21]

However, no standards exist for "chosen drinking temperature." The last standard for temperature before the consumer contacts the beverage is that for holding temperatures and recommended serving temperatures (as it is impossible to standardize the exact temperature at which a consumer contacts the beverage). Coffee cools through each stage of processing before reaching the consumer, and continues to cool while in the consumer's possession. It is neither time- nor energy-efficient to serve coffee at 130°F-140°F when consumers prefer coffee between 140°F and 160°F.[4] The result would be many requests for coffee to be reheated to a more preferred temperature and would be a waste of energy as well as both the consumer's and the barista's time. In addition to the waste of time and energy, the "breakdown of flavor will speed up if there is any fluctuation of temperature. Beverage coffee should never be allowed to cool and then be reheated."[3]

Thus, serving coffee in the hotter range of recommended serving temperatures (165°-175°F) is much more time- and energy-efficient than serving coffee at 130°-140°F, and it maintains the flavor of the coffee. This way, coffee is served so that consumers who like their coffee at 165°-175°F will be content, and those who prefer their coffee cooler can wait a minute or two before drinking the beverage (as O'Mahony's studies show, people are accustomed to wait at least thirty seconds before their first sip of the beverage). Consumers who like their coffee much cooler always have the option of requesting an ice cube or two to cool it down.

Ultimately, spilling a hot beverage is much more dangerous than drinking a hot beverage; the Brown and Diller paper is concerned with the burn danger presented by a beverage above 140°F. A spill—especially one that causes second or third degree burns—is an atypical event and is most often accidental.

It is this author's opinion that if we showered in hot coffee every day, Brown and Diller's concerns and recommendations would hold more sway. It makes a great deal more sense to use the intended and much more common experience of drinking the hot beverage as the control for holding standards and serving temperature recommendations in lieu of regulating serving temperatures based on accidental and occasional spills.

Psychological Impact of Burns

The psychological impact of burns is not as quantifiable as its physical impact. Psychological effects of burns can result from the person's reaction to their healing, scarring (pain, tightened skin, the healing process, etc.), or the loss of mobility and function in a burned, healing, or scarred body part.[19]

Shock is one of the immediate psychological impacts of a burn that might manifest in a burned person. Psychological impact on a long-term basis can be due to a number of variables. The occurrence of the burn and/or subsequent scarring and/or loss of function could affect the burned person's perception of himself or herself, and could affect his or her ability to go to work or perform everyday actions. The burned person could feel that others perceive them differently and potentially more negatively, and other people could react differently or negatively to the person's scars. These impacts of burns are intertwined.

Knowing it is Hot vs. Knowing it Burns

One claim made in hot beverage spillage lawsuits is that the consumer was not aware of the severity of the burns that hot beverages can produce. In the case of McMahon v. BUNN-O-MATIC Corporation, the plaintiffs claimed that while they knew coffee could burn, they were exposed to harm "to an extent beyond that contemplated by the ordinary consumer."[22] In the Holowaty v. McDonald's Corp. and McRick Inc., the plaintiffs claimed that McDondald's failed to "adequately warn … that severe burns could result from a spill [of a hot beverage]."[23]

In the Holowaty v. McDonald's case, the plaintiffs argued that McDonald's had a duty to warn because "the risk of injury was more severe than a reasonable consumer would anticipate." This claim was rejected by the Minnesota court hearing the case because "the type of injury the average consumer would anticipate and the injury that resulted were different in degree, not in kind".[23] In other words, the spectrum of injury possible (from a first to a third degree burn) does not change the fundamental nature of the injury (a burn, as opposed to a cut). More importantly, the court followed the logic that knowledge of the fundamental nature of an injury would cause the average consumer to assume a spectrum of injuries was possible. As applied to a hot beverage spill, the Minnesota court ruled for the defendant because it held that the risk of some burn damage was obvious to the average consumer, and thus the average consumer could assume that there was a range of burn severity possible. If there was a danger different in its fundamental nature (if coffee were extremely carcinogenic, for example), then the court would have considered that an entirely different "failure to warn."

It is clearly hard to prove that someone did not know a product is harmful, unless it appears obvious that he would have altered his actions to avoid that harm. It remains an interesting question: Does the average consumer, knowing coffee is hot, proceed down the same path of logic that the Minnesota court took, and assume a spectrum of burn severities is possible from a spill?

In a broader sense, consumers' knowledge of the product they are consuming is based on a number of factors—not least of which are warnings and disclaimers. These notices serve to provide the consumer with basic information of the hazards of certain products. No matter how many warnings are present, though, consumers must notice, read, and understand, in order to change their behavior.

CHAPTER 3

Preventive Measures:
Warnings and Spill Reactions

Before a Spill: The Warning Process

"A general tenet in human factors design is that safety should be ensured through design of the system. If the potential hazard cannot be designed out, then it should be guarded against. If guarding against the hazard is not possible, then an adequate warning system should be developed." [24]

The first defense against any dangerous aspect of a product is to eliminate the hazard. As previously discussed, however, lowering the temperature of hot beverages below a certain temperature threshold undermines both the quality of flavor and aroma. Therefore, it is not feasible to eliminate the burn hazards presented by hot beverages and maintain quality product standards.

The second defense is to guard the consumer against the hazard. To fully guard against a spill, at least three aspects of the serving environment must be examined and designed for safety.

The first step in guarding against spills is to research the cup manufacturer's products in comparison with the sizes of hot beverages offered at the location. The thickness, material, and shape of the cup should be sturdy enough to contain the greatest amount of liquid possible over time. Some cups, larger cups

especially, can weaken over time with the heat and weight of liquid and the normal structural integrity can become compromised. This outcome is obviously not desirable. Taking the time to research cups and then purchasing ones that are sturdy and heat-resistant, not only guards against a spill accident but could save money and employee time by diminishing the need to double-cup a hot beverage. In addition, how well the lid fits is critical to cup function. Again, it is very important to do the research and choose the correct lids for the cups. Lids should completely seal the cup and be easy for customers to pull on and off, but also be difficult to pop off.

Although this popular to-go cup fits human hands and car cup holders well, it is in fact top heavy and can be unstable.

Another necessary and second step—one that is often overlooked in this regard for spill prevention—is the design and layout of the café or store. How and where the customers interact with baristas and how and where customers receive the hot beverage can be optimized in many different ways in order to avoid a spill risk. For example, the traffic flow in the store can be designed so that hot beverage customers do not have to walk through crowds of other customers waiting in line. Another important aspect of customer traffic flow that can guard against a spill is correct placement of a bar or table and the condiments. The condiment table can be placed in a less-trafficked part of the store, and ideally, will be convenient to where the customer first receives the hot beverages.

What not to do: never slide coffee across the counter; it is much safer to have the server put the cup down on the counter and then have the customer pick it back up. This is also safer than serving coffee hand-to-hand.

A third important consideration is the manner in which the hot beverage is presented to the customer. This includes what products (cups and lids) the beverage is presented in and how the barista hands the beverage over to the customer. Customers at a typical café generally handle their to-go beverages in two ways: some add and mix condiments (milk, sugar, etc.) and others do not alter their hot beverages before leaving the store.

The reality of these two behaviors begs the question of whether the establishment or the customers should put lids on the cups. On one hand, when and if the customer is satisfied with an unaltered beverage, handing a customer a lidded beverage cuts out any fidgeting with the lid. However, when the customer wants to add his or her own condiments, handing a customer a lidded beverage requires the customer to handle the cup and lid much more: the customer must remove the lid, add the condiment, and reseal the lid. On the other hand, handing a customer an unlidded beverage allows the customer to see the beverage and observe signs that the beverage is hot, as well as to experience the beverage aesthetically if there are latté art garnishes or the like. The customer can choose whether to put condiments in his or her beverage and then lid it, or not. If customers lid their own drinks, they can put condiments in without first having to take off a lid. In some cases, this means the cup and lids are handled less. This mitigates the risk of human error and spills. However, the customer is more apt to make a mistake when choosing the lid size —sometimes choosing an ill-fitting lid that will leak— than is a barista.

These methods will always be prone to human error, such as the customer not putting the lid on correctly, or the barista's failure to do so. Some cafés have opted for a more intensely customer-service oriented route: if requested, they put condiments in for the customer and hand all customers a lidded beverage that does not need to be altered further. Recently, machines that seal the lids to the cups (for behind-the-counter use by employees) have appeared in various cafés and stores. This seems to be the only method of presentation that entirely removes human error, yet it could have the downside of discouraging the barista from observing and evaluating the product he or she is presenting to the customer.

Some establishments offer beverage carriers to help customers handle multiple to-go cups more safely; however, carriers can pose their own spill risks if not well constructed. Java jackets shown here provide heat protection for a person carrying the beverage.

Whether the cups are lidded or not, there are certain ways of handing a hot beverage to a customer that reduce the risk of spilling. Ideally, the beverage is placed on a counter or other surface for the customer to pick up. Avoid placing a beverage directly into a customer's hands: this prevents non-verbal miscommunication that might result in both people dropping the beverage. Also, do not slide beverages across any surface. The momentum of the cup, or the potential for the cup to become caught on the surface, greatly increases spill risk.

If a customer orders multiple hot drinks, beverage carriers (which normally carry four cups) should be available. Beverage carriers can be kept behind the counter or available at the customers' request. Placing beverages properly in these containers can be awkward or difficult, so it is suggested that baristas take the initiative to offer the carrier and place the beverages directly in the container. It can be company policy to offer or to use one automatically when a customer orders a certain number of beverages.

The third defense against a spill is to *warn the customer about the safety hazard.* This defense usually manifests as a written warning on to-go cups and/or lids. Warnings can also be posted where customers would receive hot beverages—within stores by the counter or at drive-thru windows. An option to educate the consumer and warn against the hazard is a sign posted in a café saying something like: "We serve coffee and hot beverages at temperatures exceeding 150°F, which is in accordance with industry standards for beverage quality. If you want your beverage cooler you may request that it be made cooler or for the addition of ice cubes." In addition, baristas may alert and warn customers verbally when serving them coffee or another hot beverage that has just been brewed and is hotter than if it had been held for a period of time.

The fourth line of defense would be to *prepare staff to help a customer with a spill.* Educate employees on the burn risk of hot beverages and on common burn first aid so that they may either assist a customer directly or pass this information on to a customer. It is also useful to have a checklist, as will be discussed in the next section, in order to help an employee assess and record the spill in detail.

Warning Psychology

The warning process is a complex one. There are four main steps through which a consumer might proceed after being exposed to a warning. The consumer must first **notice** the warning. Following that, the consumer must **encode** the warning. Normally, he or she then must **comprehend** the warning: the meaning of the warning is clearly understood. The last step in this process is for the consumer to **comply** with the warning.[24] Although it is easy to think of these steps as a straightforward and linear progression, some steps might not be accomplished at all and some might happen almost simultaneously or in an overlapping manner.

There are two categories of variables that control the effectiveness of a warning. The first is consumer variables, such as age, gender, and familiarity with the product. The second category includes warning variables such as color, font, size, and symbols. Because it is hard to control for how consumers approach the warning, the challenge of warning design is to manipulate the warning variables to make it easily visible, understandable, and motivating to the largest range of consumers.

Highlighted below are the variables that should be considered in the construction of a hot beverage warning.

Consumer Variables

Familiarity

Familiarity influences all four steps of the warning process. There are two opposite effects of familiarity. On one hand, familiarity with a product can lead to a greater understanding of the risks associated with the product; for example, this is usually the case with dangerous equipment where the risks of use become more apparent as the consumer's product knowledge grows.

On the other hand, familiarity with a product can lead to a lowered likelihood of consumers noticing, encoding, comprehending, and complying with the warning. Much of what the hot beverage industry does falls into this second group.

Most people are familiar with hot beverages: many people consume them multiple times a day, every day. Frequent and safe experiences with hot beverages might cause consumers to undervalue or misunderstand the warnings.[24] The thousands of times a consumer drinks coffee without spills or burns can lull him or her into a sense of safety. Such frequent, safe, and benign experiences can lower consumers' perception of risk and therefore warnings might be disregarded.

Hazard Perception

The product presents the consumer with a hazard perception level. This presentation contributes to how consumers notice, encode, and comply with the warning. If a consumer expects to encounter a dangerous product, they will be more likely to look for and/or notice a warning, and then they will be more apt to encode the warning. Increased hazard perception increases compliance.[24]

Hazard perception is particularly applicable in the hot beverage industry. Most consumers have benign experiences with the product; their first thought and expectation about hot coffee is not about being burned severely. Therefore, their hazard perception is low. This lowered perception subsequently lowers the probability that a hot beverage consumer will expect a warning, will notice, encode, and/or follow it.

Warning Variables

Signal Word

The presence of signal words such as "danger," "warning," or "caution" has proved to attract attention to the warning and to increase the likelihood that a consumer will encode and comprehend the warning.[24]

The American National Standards Institute states the standardized definitions of commonly used signal words: "DANGER: Indicates the imminently hazardous situation, which if not avoided, will result in death or serious injury. This signal word is to be limited to the most extreme situations… WARNING: Indicates a potentially hazardous situation, which if not avoided, could result in death or serious injury… CAUTION: Indicates a potentially hazardous situation that, if not avoided, may result in minor or moderate injury. It may also be used to alert against unsafe practices"[25].

The signal word "CAUTION" is typically seen in warnings on hot beverages; however, the signal word "WARNING" should be used. However infrequently burns may occur, "WARNING" is a stronger word to use in order to match the potential severity of such burns.

Symbology

There are two forms of picture-representation that can be used alone or in conjunction with a written warning: pictorials and symbols. Pictorials are explicit descriptions of the concept in an image. Symbols are abstract representations with some correlation to what they signify, but their meaning must be learned.[24]

The presence of a pictorial or symbol has been shown to affect all four steps of the warning process. The presence of a pictorial causes people to identify the presence of a warning more quickly. In terms of encoding, comprehension, and compliance, symbols are most effective when accompanied with written information.[24] There is always a possibility that the symbol used is obscure to the average consumer. Ideally, a symbol or pictorial is simple and easy to comprehend.

Explicitness

The issue of warning explicitness is of particular application in the hot beverage industry as most warnings to date are not very explicit and might only inform the consumer that the beverage is hot. Comprehension level and hazard perception are positively correlated to the explicitness of a warning. Participants in warning studies rated more explicit warnings as indicative of greater hazard.[24] Hazard perception of hot beverages can be assumed to be low for the average consumer, therefore an easy way to increase consumer hazard perception is by increasing the explicitness of hot beverage warnings. Explicitness could be improved to include information about the usual temperatures of hot beverages and how severe a resulting burn could be.

Provided response

Related to explicitness, the term "provided response" refers to whether or not the warning dictates what to do about the risk of the product. Compliance with the warning is greater if a detailed, safe response is dictated by the warning.[24] In the hot beverage industry, a provided response would have to be broad because of the multiple ways someone could spill/avoid spilling the beverage and all specific warnings would necessarily be too long and verbose. Therefore, a suggested provided response on hot beverages could be along the lines of "USE CARE."

Placement/Interactivity

The placement of the warning has been shown to influence all four steps of the warning process.[24] It poses certain challenges in the hot beverage industry, for many warnings are placed on cups and lids and need to be visible to the consumer while the consumer is holding the product. Warnings on lids are likely to be the most visible and read.

Interactivity can be incorporated into hot beverage industry warnings and has been shown to increase noticeability, encoding, and compliance.[24] A warning could be placed on the lid so a consumer must remove it before sipping the beverage. However, this is a rather in-your-face warning technique, and the hazards of a hot beverage might not merit that extreme warning placement.

Another example of interactivity can be seen in a lid that the Smart Lid company has developed.[26] This lid changes from a darker to a lighter color as the beverage's temperature changes and shows whether the seal around the lid is broken or secure. This technology has yet to be employed by major hot beverage companies.

Warning labels can be found on both home and commercial coffee brewers, such as this Keurig single-cup coffee brewer.

Standardization/Variability in Warnings:

Industry-wide warning guidelines would help to influence the encoding and comprehension of hot beverage warnings. The techniques of standardization and variability have been applied in the tobacco and alcohol industries, and in experimental studies have been shown to have a positive effect on encoding and compliance. Varying the content of warning labels on alcohol products resulted in increased encoding and compliance with the warning.[24] Researchers caution, however, that standardization might lead to increased familiarity with warnings and cause consumer habituation.[24] An interesting way of combating habituation to standardized warnings would be to vary the information contained in the warning but keep other aspects of the warning constant. For example, the text of the warning could vary, but where it is printed on the cup and/or lid, as well as the colors, text, and format used could remain the same.

Applied Warning Psychology: Hot Beverage Warnings

Many dimensions of warnings are discussed in warning psychology literature. Two dimensions that apply when writing a warning are (a) the purpose of the warning and (b) the criteria by which success or failure in achieving the purpose(s) is measured.[27] Currently, most warnings are for informing the consumer that the beverage is hot. However, warnings' failures or successes are very hard to measure with such generic language. In other more explicit warnings with a provided response to the risk, it is easier to display the purpose of the warning and therefore judge whether the warning succeeded or failed.

A warning must be short, simple, and expressive, and must accomplish three things: (1) attract attention, so the consumer *notices* and *encodes* the warning, (2) inform, so the consumer *comprehends* the warning, and (3) motivate, so the consumer *complies* with the warning.

Examples of hard-to-read warnings on lids.

Attract attention: placement, signal word, typography, color

The warning should be optimally placed on the to-go cup and/or lid, the signal word of the warning should be noticeable and prominent, and the typography and colors used should stand out from the background.

Inform fully and succinctly: signal word, severity of risk, immediacy of risk

In the case of the burn danger, the warning should have a signal word followed by the risk posed, the severity of the burn possible, and the immediacy of the burn damage. It is necessary to keep in mind the range of consumers who will encounter the warning and to avoid industry or medical jargon that is not descriptive to the public.

Motivate:

The term "motivate" as applied to a warning is defined by this question: "Does this product threaten the average consumer and compel him or her to use the product responsibly?" The motivational impact of a warning is measured by how effective it is at attracting attention and informing the consumer of the possible risk.

Examples of warnings on cups.

There is some debate over how graphic a warning on a cup/lid should be. It should be graphic enough to motivate the consumer to treat the beverage with caution, but not so graphic that it has the potential to disturb or discourage the consumer from enjoying the beverage. It is best to walk the line with a phrase that conveys the risk of severe burns without much extraneous medical detail.

An example of an acceptable warning on a cup or lid that takes all of these parameters into account is:

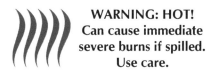 **WARNING: HOT!**
Can cause immediate
severe burns if spilled.
Use care.

Drive-thru windows pose several spill risks. One primary issue is that many car windows are at a level lower than the establishment's drive-thru window and result in a precarious beverage hand-off.

The first part of the warning—"WARNING: HOT!"—uses the appropriate signal word for risk and introduces the most basic danger, namely the heat of the beverage. The phrase, "can cause immediate severe burns," adds to the immediacy and the severity of the risk, informing the consumer more fully. It is possible to say something like: "Can cause immediate third degree burns requiring skin grafts." Although this is more explanatory, it contains medical terminology such as "third degree" and "skin grafts" that might not be understood by everyone. The last part of the warning—"use care"—gives an adequate, though vague, provided response, as it would be too lengthy and presumptuous to detail how to follow the warning in an encompassing and specific manner.

Symbols or pictorials usually come to the left of the written warning, or are separated from the written warning in some way. In a brief survey of warnings used in the coffee industry, symbols or pictorials are not commonly included with a warning about the hot beverage.

Examples of current warnings on counters or drive-through windows:

CAUTION: Coffee, Tea, and Hot Chocolate are served VERY HOT.

Examples of current warnings on cups:

Currently, warnings are usually placed in the bottom half-inch of the cup, and/ or at the top of the sleeve. The warnings either are printed once, twice, or are repeated all around the cup.

Careful, the beverage you're about to enjoy is extremely hot.

CAUTION: HOT CONTENTS

CAUTION: HANDLE WITH CARE I'M HOT

CAUTION: THIS BEVERAGE IS EXTREMELY HOT

CAUTION: VERY HOT

CAUTION: HOT

Examples of current warnings on lids:

Warnings are usually printed on both the cup and the lid. Warnings on the lid curve around the edge of the lid, or are printed in the center of the lid. In both cases, the warning usually faces the area of the lid from which a person would drink.

WARNING HOT!

CAUTION! CONTENTS HOT!

CAUTION CONTENTS HOT

CAUTION I'M HOT

CAUTION HOT

Warnings on cups and lids in the US are always in English, sometimes in Spanish, and occasionally in French. Symbols used in current warnings are a flame with the word "HOT!" inside it or an image of evaporation and/or evaporation from a cup (*see Appendix*).

After a Spill: First Aid and Recording the Incident

Despite all of these precautions, a spill can still occur. If a spill happens, there are two main steps to take.

Step 1: Help the injured party.

Ask permission to help the injured party.

If he or she does not want to be helped, inform the injured party to remove any articles of clothing that have absorbed the hot liquid as fast as possible, and tell the person about burn first aid.

If the person gives consent to be helped…

Help him or her remove the hazard. This is very important if a hot beverage was spilled onto clothing, for example. The clothing could absorb the hot liquid and keep it close to the person's skin, thus increasing the amount of time his or her skin is in contact with the hot liquid, and increasing the burn severity.

Once the hazard has been removed from the burn area…

Give the injured party direct first aid or information about what first aid is effective. The essential point in burn first aid is that placing the burn under cool (not ice-cold) water for twenty minutes helps to ameliorate the severity of the burn. This can be done up to an hour after the incident with the same effect.

Get the contact information of the injured party, if possible.

Step 2: Assess and Record the incident as soon as possible.

Check temperatures and settings of all machines involved in the production of the drink as soon as possible following a spill.

Capture anything such as the cup or lid involved, if possible.

Take photographs of the incident and/or the location of the incident, the machine involved, and the cup (if any) involved, as soon as possible.

Record a written statement of what happened. Include in this statement the time of the incident, the machine used to make the beverage, the machine's model number etc., and the temperatures/settings of the machine. Also include any behavior of the employee serving the customer and the employee's first knowledge of and reaction to the spill.

Give this report to supervisors and/or managers, and keep the report on file.

Step 3: Follow up with the injured party and show concern for their well-being. Although contact with the person after the incident is not guaranteed, it is a good idea to be helpful during the spill and to reach out and show concern for the customer after the incident. However, a retailer may have other policies regarding contact with an injured party.

CHAPTER 4

Brew and Sue:
Hot Beverage Litigation

Lessons from Past Cases

Most hot beverage litigation involves coffee or tea. Ten out of the thirteen cases listed in detail here involved coffee, two involved tea, and one involved the spill of a latté. The American to-go culture of drive-thrus, beverage trays, to-go cups with lids, and consumption of hot beverages in vehicles contributed to nearly every case.

Nine out of the thirteen cases listed in this manual involved a spill that occurred in a car. Spills mostly occur in cars due to the physical restrictions—the lack of holders or flat surfaces and the movement of the vehicle. Drivers as well as passengers spill beverages. While a car is stationary, both driver and passenger could have little to no storage or surface space for beverages, an experience that could contribute to a spill. Driver and passenger are also contained within the car seat in such a way that it is difficult to move to avoid a spill. While the car is moving, the physical restrictions in the car compound with curves, bumps, hills, and distracting traffic situations to create a perfect storm of spill variables—a driver might well be paying more attention to the roads and traffic, thus handling the hot beverage with less caution and attention, or a passenger might not be attuned to the abrupt movements of the car. In almost all car spill cases, the spills occurred because of movement of the car and/or the plaintiff's attempt to remove the lid to add condiments. Therefore, it is critical for companies serving beverages from drive-thrus and in to-go cups to be aware of the to-go culture's hot beverage spill risks and to put preventative measures in place, such as those discussed in this paper.

In none of the hot beverage litigation recorded did the author find temperature information from immediately before or after the spill occurred. The plaintiffs in these cases can only prove how severely they were burned. Although the variability of burn depth is based on factors in addition to temperature, the exact temperature of beverages involved in spills seems not to have been known or recorded. The recommended serving temperatures and preferred drinking temperatures of hot beverages are above both the skin pain threshold and the burn damage threshold. This reality will always exist in this industry unless consumer preferences change drastically or a way of optimizing taste at lower temperatures is discovered. *Accordingly, the fact that spills cause burns is not proof that beverages were unreasonably hot and dangerous.*

In the 1994 case of *Liebeck v. McDonald's Inc.,* Mrs. Stella Liebeck originally only wanted McDonald's to cover the cost of her medical bills[28]. McDonald's ended up picking the wrong fight; they spent much more money defending themselves in the lawsuit and even more in payment as a result of losing the lawsuit. For companies who are being sued, it is worth considering, early on, whether to fight a claim or lawsuit. A business should choose wisely by examining what happened and then deciding whether a claim can be successfully contested. Claims that the beverage was "too hot" and other claims pinning liability to the beverage temperature have been successfully contested with the help of an expert witness knowledgeable as to the proper temperatures needed for a quality hot beverage.

Failure to warn claims can largely be avoided by improving warnings on cups, lids, trays, sleeves, and delivery surfaces. These warnings can range from "HOT!" and "CAUTION: CONTENTS HOT" to a more explicit and detailed warning, such as the one recommended on page 66.

Frivolous Lawsuits

Media coverage of the case of *Liebeck v. McDonald's* created a stir throughout the country in 1994. It became commonly known that a woman was awarded millions of dollars in a lawsuit after she spilled a cup of coffee on her lap and sustained burns. A few lawsuits pertaining to hot beverage spills occurred before *Liebeck*, but the amount of litigation involving hot beverage spills after 1995 has been much greater. This could be a factor of an increasingly litigious society, as well as the widespread knowledge of the *Liebeck* verdict.

Seventeen years after the *Liebeck* case, Susan Saladoff, a former plaintiff's attorney, directed the documentary *Hot Coffee*.[29] The documentary presents the facts of the *Liebeck* case as a rebuttal to the "common knowledge" that it was a frivolous lawsuit. Saladoff uses the *Liebeck* case and other cases to highlight the negative side of tort reform and its infringements on an individual's right to go to court. (Although this manual is concerned with the distinction between frivolous and legitimate lawsuits, it is not meant as a commentary on tort reform.)

The term "frivolous" is often connected with hot beverage litigation even though these cases were not found frivolous by the court system. "Frivolous" serves both as an English word and as legal jargon. A "frivolous idea", for example, is an idea that lacks substance or merit. A "frivolous claim" in legal jargon refers to an entire lawsuit or motions within a lawsuit that are "intended to harass, delay or embarrass the opposition" and it "lacks any [legal] basis"[30]. In current hot beverage lawsuits, because of the media's pervasive reporting on *Liebeck*, it is difficult to ascertain whether the plaintiff was truly surprised by the severity of the injury or the plaintiff was motivated by knowledge of the financial award in the Liebeck case.

The vast majority of hot beverage litigation claims center on the assertion that the beverage spilled was too hot for human consumption and thus unreasonably dangerous. In *Hot Coffee*, Saladoff conducts interviews about the *Liebeck* case with people she encounters on the street. She contrasts the assumptions they had from media coverage of the case with their reactions to the severity of the injury after viewing photographs of Ms. Liebeck's burns. The common surprise that a coffee spill can cause severe burns drives many claims that coffee is too hot. The burns that people sustain from hot beverages are real and painful, but *that does not legitimize claims that beverages were served too hot or were unreasonably dangerous. The same beverages could have been consumed without incident—and without injury lawsuits—if the consumers involved had used reasonable care, knowing that coffee is hot and therefore dangerous.*

Common Claims

Common claims in hot beverage cases are negligence and breach of warranty of fitness for a particular purpose and breach of warranty of merchantability. To prove these products liability claims, the product must be found to be defective in its design, manufacturing, or marketing.[31] Hot beverage cases usually involve design defect claims (the coffee was "excessively hot" and therefore defective) and defective marketing claims, such as failure to warn. Plaintiffs in hot beverage litigation cases may seek to apply the principle of *res ipsa loquitor* to the incident.

The principle of *res ipsa loquitor*: The Latin translation is "the thing speaks for itself." This principle permits plaintiffs to meet their burden of proof with circumstantial evidence. *Res ipsa loquitor* is only applicable if the plaintiff can show that the injury/accident was under the defendant's control, that it could only have happened through negligence on the part of the defendant, and that the plaintiff's actions were not a factor in the accident.[36]

Possible products liability claims:

Negligence: Negligence is defined as "a failure to behave with the level of care that someone of ordinary prudence would have exercised under the same circumstance."[32]

Strict liability (in products liability cases): Anytime a defective product under the defendant's responsibility causes injury to the plaintiff, regardless of intent of the defendant.[33]

Breach of warranty of fitness for a particular purpose: The warranty of fitness for a particular purpose is implied in a transaction where the seller and buyer both assume the product sold is to be used for a particular and identical reason.[34]

Breach of warranty of merchantability: The warranty of merchantability is an implied guarantee to a consumer that the product purchased fit the standards of quality and was adequately packaged and labeled.[35]

A Walk through Common Claims involved in Hot Coffee Litigation, via the Holowaty v. McDonald's Inc. Decision [21]

Below is a walk-through of the *Holowaty v. McDonald's Inc.* decision.[23] This case includes claims commonly involved in hot coffee litigation.

Facts of *Holowaty v. McDonald's Corp.*, 10 F. Supp. 2d 1078 (D. Minn. 1998):

- Mr. and Mrs. Holowaty, Plaintiffs
- McDonald's Inc and McRick Inc., Defendants
- The Plaintiffs drank two to three cups of coffee per day.
- At McDonald's in Rochester, Minnesota, Plaintiffs went into the restaurant (not drive-thru).
- They ordered a "large cup of coffee."
- The coffee and juice were placed in a beverage tray.
- The coffee was in a Styrofoam cup covered by a lid.
- The styrofoam cup and lid had "HOT!" and "CAUTION: CONTENTS HOT" warnings.
- The beverages were placed in a beverage tray by a McDonald's employee and then handed to Mr. Holowaty.
- The lift-tab of the coffee cup lid was opened by Mr. Holowaty before exiting the restaurant.
- Once in the car, Mrs. Holowaty sat in the passenger's seat with the beverage tray in her lap.
- When exiting the parking lot, they drove down a steep decline.
- The coffee tipped and spilled about half its contents onto Mrs. Holowaty's lap.
- The coffee soaked into Mrs. Holowaty's shorts.
- The coffee caused second-degree burns to her upper and inner thighs.
- The burns took two months to heal, leaving permanent scars.
- The Holowatys filed suit against McRick Inc, the owner of the McDonald's restaurant, and McDonald's the franchisor.
- The Plaintiffs contended that the coffee was defective because it was excessively hot and that the Defendants did not provide adequate warnings about the severity of the burns that could result from a spill.

Holowaty vs. McDonald's was resolved by summary judgment in favor of the Defendants. The following information on the case and the summary judgment is taken from the memorandum opinion and order granting summary judgment motion.[21]

Strict Liability: Design defect and failure to warn claims

Design defect claim:

The argument used by the Plaintiff for this claim was that the coffee served was a defective product because it was "excessively hot." The Defendants countered that argument by saying that heat (to the extent that the heat of the coffee contributed to the incident) was inherent to the quality of a cup of coffee. The judge used two legal tests to evaluate the Plaintiff's design defect claim, the **consumer expectations test** and the **reasonable care balancing test**. The consumer expectations test is one that is applied to something such as a beverage or other food item, whereas the reasonable care balancing test is usually applied to non-edible products. The Defense argued for use of the consumer expectations test, and the Plaintiff argued for use of the reasonable care balancing test. To be thorough and to satisfy the requests of both parties, the judge performed both tests. The incident failed to pass either one.

The incident failed to pass the consumer expectations test because the Plaintiffs presented no evidence that the coffee was hotter than normal and thus harm from the heat of the coffee could be expected by the reasonable consumer.

The incident failed to pass the reasonable care balancing test because the Defendants "presented evidence that heat is an essential element of a quality cup of coffee."

Failure to warn claim:

"Plaintiffs contend that the coffee was defective because it was not accompanied by adequate warnings."

The Defendants contended they didn't have a duty to warn "because the danger of burns [from coffee] is open and obvious." The judge held it common knowledge that the average consumer knows coffee is hot and thus poses a burn risk. Not only is the risk of burns argued as common knowledge, but the judge also stated the risk as analogous to the type of obvious danger posed by a sharp knife, with the dangerous aspect being inherent to the quality of the product. The Plaintiffs had stated in the proceedings that they were aware that hot coffee can cause burns, which was used by the judge as more evidence towards the burn risk being common knowledge.

The judge rejected the duty portion of the failure to warn claim because the "type of injury the average consumer would anticipate and the injury that resulted were different in degree, not in kind." It is common sense that the average consumer postulates a range of possible risk from anything potentially dangerous. If the risk were derived from a different source of danger, a warning would be necessary to inform the average consumer. For example, a range of possible burn degrees could be assumed from a contact with hot liquid – an injury different in degree – but if the hot liquid were also carcinogenic, an injury sustained would be different in kind.

The Defendants also contended the Plaintiffs had insufficient proof that the alleged inadequacy of the warning *caused* the injuries. To successfully claim that warning inadequacy caused the incident, the Plaintiffs would have needed to show that they would have acted differently, taking heed of the hypothetical warning. The judge stated that the Plaintiffs "knowingly took the coffee into a moving vehicle, compounding the danger. A reasonable person taking hot coffee into a car would handle the coffee with care. Thus, even if Defendants had included a warning … there is no reason to believe that Plaintiffs would have altered their conduct."

At this point, the author would like to note that this particular claim would not have been up for debate had the Defendants included a more detailed and effective warning, as discussed in the Preventative Measures chapter of this manual.

General Liability: Negligence and Implied Warranty of Merchantability

The Plaintiffs failed to prove the product defective in the claims discussed above. For the "implied warrant of merchantability" to be breached, the product needed to be proven defective.

In *Holowaty v. McDonald's*, these two claims were viewed by the court as more general than the stricter liability issues addressed in the failure to warn and the defective design claims; because the stricter liability claims had failed to support the Plaintiffs arguments, the general ones were considered not applicable as well.

Your Defense: Your Expert Witness(es)

An expert witness is someone who "by reasons of education or special training, possesses knowledge of some particular subject area in greater depth than the public at large."[37] Expert witnesses are brought into the court to give opinions on matters concerning the case at hand.

It is essential to prepare expert witnesses for all parts of the legal process. They should be familiarized with phrasing their answers in ways that maintain their credibility and do not extend beyond the scope of their expertise. Expert witnesses should be prepared to resist being swayed by leading questions and other devices used to undermine their credibility. Several books discuss in detail the recommendations for expert witnesses, one of which is *Effective Expert Witnessing* by Jack V. Matson.

Overview, Claims, and Outcomes of Hot Beverage Lawsuits

1985: Huppe v. Twenty-First Century Restaurants of Am., Inc., 130 Misc. 2d 736, 497 N.Y.S.2d 306 (Sup. Ct. 1985) aff'd, 116 A.D.2d 797, 498 N.Y.S.2d 332 (1986):[38]

Plaintiff: Female

Beverage: Coffee

Beverage temperature: Unknown

Spill environment: Passenger seat of car

Plaintiff involvement in spill: Beverage spilled while under control of the plaintiff

Activity that caused spill: Removal of lid to add condiments in addition to movement of car

Burn area: Chest, neck, face, shoulders

Burn degree: First and second degree burns

CLAIMS:

Products liability, failure to warn

Negligence and breach of warranty for serving coffee at too high a temperature

OUTCOME:

Defendant's motion for summary judgment was granted. Product held to be not defective or unusually dangerous, and there was no failure to warn.

* * * *

1994: Lamkin v. Braniff Airlines, Inc., 853 F. Supp. 30 (D. Mass. 1994):[39]

Plaintiff: Female

Beverage: Coffee

Beverage temperature: Unknown

Spill environment: Plane

Plaintiff involvement in spill: Beverage spilled onto Plaintiff

Activity that caused spill: Movement of plane seat in front of Plaintiff

Burn area: Thighs, lap

Burn degree: Second and third degree

CLAIMS:

Negligence in hiring, in instructing flight personnel in serving hot beverages, and in how to provide first aid

Negligence: Failure to warn about the temperature of the beverage

Negligence: Failure to warn about the hazards of moving a seat

OUTCOME:

Defendant's motion for summary judgment granted. There was no negligence shown, no failure to warn, and the doctrine of res ipsa loquitor was not applicable.

1994: Liebeck v. McDonald's Restaurants, P.T.S., Inc., CV-93-02419, 1995 WL 360309 (N.M. Dist. Aug. 18, 1994) vacated sub nom. Liebeck v. Restaurants, CV-93-02419, 1994 WL 16777704 (N.M. Dist. Nov. 28, 1994):[28]

Plaintiff: 79-year-old female

Beverage: Coffee

Beverage temperature: Unknown

Spill environment: Passenger seat of car, drive-thru

Plaintiff involvement in spill: Plaintiff spilled beverage

Activity that caused spill: Plaintiff put cup of coffee between her legs in a parked car. In an attempt to get the lid off of the cup, she spilled coffee onto her lap.

Burn area: Abdomen, groin

Burn degree: Second and third degree

CLAIM(S):

The coffee was "excessively hot," and thus "unreasonably dangerous." The coffee itself was "defectively manufactured" because of the "excessive heat" and the container had "design defects" and was "defectively marked," lacking warnings. Claims against Defendants included products liability and breach of warranty, and that the Defendants sold a defective product.

OUTCOME:

The jury found for the Plaintiff as to her claims of product defect, breach of implied warranty, and breach of the implied warranty of fitness for a particular purpose. The jury found the Plaintiff 20% at fault and awarded $160,000 in compensatory damages, and $2.7 million in punitive damages.

1997: *Nadel v. Burger King Corp.*, **119 Ohio App. 3d 578, 695 N.E.2d 1185 (1997)** *overruled by Bouher v. Aramark Servs., Inc.*, **2009-Ohio-1597, 181 Ohio App. 3d 599, 910 N.E.2d 40:** [40]

Plaintiff: Male child

Beverage: Coffee, two cups in a beverage tray

Beverage temperature: Unknown

Spill environment: Passenger seat of car, drive-thru

Plaintiff involvement in spill: Beverage was in control of the plaintiff

Activity that caused spill: Supposed movement of the car

Burn area: Foot

Burn degree: Second degree

CLAIMS:

Breach of warranty of merchantability

Breach of warranty of fitness for a particular purpose

Product liability for a defective product

Failure to warn

OUTCOME:

The Court held that there was no intervening superseding cause. Summary judgment for defendant was granted regarding claims for breach of warranty of merchantability and fitness for particular purpose, as well as for claims of negligence toward business invitees and negligent infliction of emotional distress. Summary judgment for Defendant was not granted with regard to claims of design defect and failure to warn. Summary judgment for Defendant also was not granted on the question of punitive damages.

However, Bouher v. Aramark Servs., Inc. overruled Nadel, and held that summary judgment for defendant can be granted in a case where an obviously hot liquid like coffee or tea spills on a plaintiff because the hot liquid presents an open and obvious risk.

* * * *

1998: *Holowaty v. McDonald's Corp.,* **10 F. Supp. 2d 1078 (D. Minn. 1998):**[23]
Please refer to prior section for an extensive review of this case.

Plaintiff: Female

Beverage: Coffee, in beverage tray

Beverage temperature: Unknown

Spill environment: Passenger seat of car

Plaintiff involvement in spill: The beverage spilled while under control of the Plaintiff

Activity that caused spill: Movement of the car

Burn area: Thighs and groin

Burn degree: Second degree

ADDITIONAL NARRATIVE: The Plaintiff was carrying a beverage tray with a juice and a large coffee in her lap while in the passenger seat of her car. When the car went down a steep decline and the tray tipped, the coffee spilt onto her lap.

CLAIMS:

Beverage was defective because it was excessively hot.

The Defendants did not provide adequate warnings about the severity of the burns that could result from a spill.

OUTCOME:

Defendants' motion for summary judgment on all four of the Plaintiff's claims was granted: the Court held that there was no design defect, no failure to warn, no negligence, and no implied warranty of merchantability.

* * * *

1998: *McMahon v. Bunn-O-Matic Corp.,* **150 F.3d 651 (7th Cir. 1998):** [41]

Plaintiff: Female

Beverage: Coffee, Styrofoam cup

Beverage temperature: Unknown

Spill environment: Passenger seat of car

Plaintiff involvement in spill: The beverage spilled while under control of the Plaintiff

Activity that caused spill: Plaintiff's handling of coffee

Burn area: Left thigh, lower abdomen

Burn degree: Second and third degree

ADDITIONAL NARRATIVE: The plaintiff was sitting in the passenger seat of a car. The Plaintiff attempted to pour the coffee into a smaller cup and then the coffee spilled onto her lap.

CLAIMS:

Products liability, duty to warn, and design defect

OUTCOME:

Defendants' motion for summary judgment was upheld on appeal regarding both product defect claim and failure to warn claims.

* * * *

2003: *Wurtzel v. Starbucks Coffee Co.*, 257 F. Supp. 2d 520 (E.D.N.Y. 2003): [42]

Plaintiff: 43-year-old female

Beverage: Coffee, 20 oz.

Beverage temperature: Unknown

Spill environment: Driver's seat, while driving

Plaintiff involvement in spill: Beverage was under control of Plaintiff when spill occurred

Activity that caused spill: Movement of the car

Burn area: Right thigh and leg

Burn degree: Second degree

ADDITIONAL NARRATIVE: Plaintiff placed the beverage in the cup holder of her car. While she was making a turn, the coffee spilled into the seat, although the cup allegedly never tipped over or exited the cup holder.

CLAIMS:

Negligence

OUTCOME:

Defendant's motion for summary judgment was granted on claim of negligence, and the res ipsa loquitor theory of liability was ruled inapplicable.

* * * *

2009: *Moltner v. Starbucks Coffee Co.*, 624 F.3d 34 (2d Cir. 2010): [43]

Plaintiff: 76-yr-old female

Beverage: Tea, 20 oz. cup, double-cupped

Beverage temperature: Unknown

Spill environment: Table inside café

Plaintiff involvement in spill: Plaintiff spilled beverage

Activity that caused spill: Taking lid off to add condiments

Burn area: Foot

Burn degree: First and allegedly second degree

ADDITIONAL NARRATIVE: Upon taking off the lid of her double-cupped "venti"-sized tea, hot water spilled on Plaintiff's foot, soaking into her sneaker.

CLAIMS:

Products liability

Negligence

Failure to warn

OUTCOME:

District Court's grant of summary judgment for defendant was upheld on appeal. Claims for design defect and negligence both failed.

2010: *Colbert v. Sonic Restaurants, Inc.*, 741 F. Supp. 2d 764 (W.D. La. 2010): [44]

Plaintiff: 50-year-old male

Beverage: Coffee

Beverage temperature: Unknown

Spill environment: Driver's seat of car, parked, drive-thru

Plaintiff involvement in spill: Plaintiff spilled beverage

Activity that caused spill: Taking lid off to add condiments

Burn area: Abdomen, groin

Burn degree: First and allegedly second degree

ADDITIONAL NARRATIVE: The plaintiff spilled coffee into his lap after going through a drive-thru and parking to take the lid off and put condiments in the coffee. The coffee soaked into his jeans and underwear but he didn't change until he had driven home. He sustained first and allegedly second degree burns in lower stomach and groin.

CLAIMS:

Products liability

Inadequate warning

Negligence

Coffee unreasonably dangerous due to it being too hot and the cup filled too high.

OUTCOME:

Defendant's motion for summary judgment granted on all counts.

Cases That Were Settled Outside of Court

Case A:

Beverage: Coffee, 16oz, Styrofoam cup

Beverage Temperature: Unknown

Spill environment: Driver's seat of car, while driving, after having gone through the drive-thru

Plaintiff involvement in spill: The beverage spilled while under control of the plaintiff

Activity that caused spill: Movement of the car

Burn area: Right ankle and right leg

Burn degree: Second degree

Plaintiff held the coffee in one hand as he drove due to a lack of cup holders in his car that would accommodate the size of the cup. Coffee spilled onto his thigh when going over a bump in the road, which caused him to twist the cup and jerk the cup away. The lid allegedly came off at that time and dumped the rest of the coffee onto his lap.

Case B:

Beverage: Latté

Beverage Temperature: Unknown

Spill environment: Delivery surface at café counter

Plaintiff involvement in spill: Plaintiff and employee were allegedly both holding the beverage

Activity that caused spill: Plaintiff's attempt to check how secure the lid was on the beverage

Burn area: Wrist

Burn degree: First and second degree

A latté was handed to the woman, although it is unclear whether it was picked up by her or handed by the server to the woman in mid-air. The Plaintiff was burned on her right wrist as a result of trying to secure the lid of the coffee cup which she claimed was not on correctly. She had skin grafts for the 1st and 2nd degree burns.

Case C:

Beverage: Coffee, 16oz cup with sleeve and lid, 12oz cup with sleeve and lid

Beverage Temperature: Unknown

Spill environment: Driver's seat of car (stationary)

Plaintiff involvement in spill: The beverages were under control of the Plaintiff

Activity that caused spill: Plaintiff's attempt to take beverages out of cup holders

Burn area: Thighs and groin

Burn degree: Second degree

Plaintiff left both cups of coffee in cup holders of the car while running errands before returning home. Plaintiff returned home and upon taking both beverages in her hands, spilled some onto her thighs and then dropped both cups onto her lap.

Case D:

Beverage: Tea, 12oz cup

Beverage Temperature: Unknown

Spill environment: Delivery surface inside café

Plaintiff involvement in spill: Allegedly did not touch the cup of tea prior to or during the spill

Activity that caused spill: Allegedly poor service in delivering the drink (sliding it on the counter)

Burn area: Abdomen

Burn degree: First and allegedly second degree

A 12oz tea spilled onto the Plaintiff's abdomen from the delivery surface; it is unclear if the spill resulted due to server negligence (pushing the beverage towards the customer) or if the cup or lid disintegrated. There were no witnesses to the accident. An ambulance crew came to the scene and administered first aid but the Plaintiff refused to go to the hospital.

CLAIMS:

Negligence; the store employee was 100% negligent. Plaintiff made no claim that the temperature of the water exceeded industry standards.

Other Relevant Cases

Terrance v. Brother's Gourmet Coffee, Denver District Court 96-CV-3848, November 1997

Patino v. McDonald's Corporation, San Bernardino Superior Court SCV 30702, March 1998

Shea v. Starbucks Coffee Company, Los Angeles Superior Court, SC 035264, March 1998

Leu v. McDonald's Corporation, Iowa District Court, LACV 020958, November 1998

Addams v FMC and Sysco, 3rd Judicial Court, Civil No. 960907227PI, Salt Lake County Utah, July 1999

Brown v. Carl Karcher Enterprises, Inc. San Bernandino Superior Court, SCV 58158, February 2001

McCroy v. Coastal Mart and Curits, U.S. District Court, Kansas, 99-1090-MLB, August 2001

Prados v. Imperial Palace, et al, District Court, Clark County Nevada, Nevada Case #A428324,February 2005

Casebolt v. McDonald's et al, District Court 4th Judicial District, Idaho Case # CV PI 0802784, February 2010

Avila v. Sweet Treats, Inc. et al, Lake Superior Court, Indiana Case # 45D02-0809-CT-00259, October 2011

Conclusion

In an ideal world, no one would be injured by knives, stovetops, burners, cars, or any other hazards with which risk is inherent in their function. Millions of people drink coffee and other hot beverages safely every day, yet it is inevitable that spills happen.

Handling Hot Coffee presents a foundation of information and recommendations to help protect consumers and companies from spills, burns, and resulting lawsuits. This manual brings together the heretofore scattered information relevant to hot beverage lawsuits–material pulled from the diverse fields of hot beverage food science, medical knowledge of burns, warning psychology and products liability. By consolidating the pertinent information, *Handling Hot Coffee* provides the necessary knowledge and tools to foster a corporate and consumer culture of spill and burn prevention.

This manual's first section on industry standards distinguishes the product, the serving process, and person (server) as elements in the creation of an enjoyable beverage. The same elements affect spill, burn, and lawsuit prevention. The "product" aspect of prevention includes the beverage and its packaging. The beverage's temperature should be within the specifications outlined in this paper. Machines involved in making hot beverages should be checked regularly to ensure that temperatures are within specifications. Cups, lids, sleeves, and trays should be tested for how securely they contain the hot beverages and should display abundant warnings. The "process" aspect of prevention details the concerns and issues involved in delivering hot beverages safely. The design of the café or drive-thru should be set up to minimize spill risk. Company policies should be in place for handling and documenting a spill. The "people" aspect of prevention involves training servers how to deliver a hot beverage safely—placing it on the delivery surface (e.g. counters, tabletops, etc.) or using care to deliver a beverage through a drive-thru window. Servers of hot beverages should also be trained in how to handle a spill: employees should assist the customer, recommend first aid, and then fill out forms to document the incident.

Companies that seek to serve the highest quality beverages should follow the temperature guidelines enumerated in this paper. However, as some lawsuits seek to claim, it may be the responsibility of the companies serving hot beverages to take precautionary measures such as the ones recommended in this manual. Whether or not it is the legal duty of hot beverage companies to take precautionary measures against spills, this manual's author advocates prudence and that companies consider precautionary measures as their responsibility.

Handling Hot Coffee
Preventing Spills, Burns, and Lawsuits
Summary of Recommendations:

BEVERAGE TEMPERATURES:

Coffee

BREWED *at* 195–205° F

HELD *at* 175–185° F

SERVED *at* 165–175° F

Tea

STEEPED *at* 200–210° F

Steamed Milk Beverages

STEAMED *to* 150–160° F

BURN FIRST AID:

Run cool water over the burned area for 20 minutes.

WARNING SUGGESTION:

WARNING: HOT! Can cause immediate severe burns if spilled. Use care.

PREVENTATIVE STEPS:

1. Educate employees on the burn risk of hot beverages and on proper responses (first aid and other) to customer spills and burns.

2. Train employees on how to interact with and hand beverages to customers to foster the safest possible spill-free environment.

3. Encourage employees to verbally express hot beverage warnings in person to customers.

4. Use cups, lids, trays, and sleeves that are sturdy and hold their shape even when containing hot liquids. Test these materials with drinks and delivery surfaces.

5. Put multiple warnings in visible places on cups, lids, trays, sleeves and delivery surfaces.

6. Carefully examine the process of serving the beverages. Consider whether to put the lid on for the customer, whether to put condiments in for the customer, and whether to alter this process for drive-thrus or other delivery surfaces.

Handling Hot Coffee
Preventing Spills, Burns, and Lawsuits
Summary of Recommendations:

AFTER A SPILL:

1. Offer first aid to the injured party.

2. Get the facts surrounding a spill as quickly as possible. These include: temperature settings of machines involved, exact time and location of the spill, which employees served the customer, exact statement of the injured party, whether the customer was a new or repeat customer, employee(s) statement of what happened, possible video or surveillance tape of the incident, and any bystanders' accounts of what happened.

3. Have a representative from the machine company or an outside party come and verify temperatures from the machine(s) involved and whether the machines were working correctly.

4. Keep track of any communication with the injured party. If possible, acquire copies of all doctor's reports.

5. Keep all of this paperwork on file.

AFTER A CLAIM IS MADE OR A LAWSUIT IS FILED:

1. Decide whether to settle or contest the claim. Cases involving the spill by an employee onto a customer generally should be settled. However, hot beverage spills that involve the plaintiff being in charge of the beverage during the spill – especially claims of the spill involving an unreasonably dangerous hot beverage – threaten the quality standards of the hot beverage industry and should be contested.

2. Prepare a strong defense with at least one expert witness who can testify authoritatively on temperatures needed for the preparation of quality of hot beverages.

Beverage Temperature and Burn Threshold Summary

Temperature in °F: 100 · 105 · 110 · 115 · 120 · 125 · 130 · 135 · 140 · 145 · 150 · 155 · 160 · 165 · 170 · 175 · 180 · 185 · 190 · 195 · 200 · 205 · 210 · 215 · 220 · 225 · 230

Reference temperatures
- Hot tub water 100–104°F
- Home hot water heater 120°F
- Boiling water 212°F
- Steam

Pain & burn thresholds
- Skin pain threshold 107.6–109.4°F
- Burn damage threshold 130–135°F
- Above skin pain and burn damage thresholds

3rd degree burns acquired at x temp.
- 3rd degree burns @ 133°F in 15 sec
- 3rd degree burns @ 140°F in 5 sec
- 3rd degree burns @ 149°F in 2 sec
- 3rd degree burns @ 150°F within 1 second

Consumer preferences for serving temperatures (O'Mahoney Studies)
- Preferred drinking temp. 139.6°F
- Preferred sipping temp. 161.8°F
- Most expected serving temp 165°F
- Average temp (black) at first sip 168°F

Industry standards for brewing and holding hot coffee
- Recommended serving temp 165–175°F
- Holding temp range 175–185°F
- Home brewer holding range (2 min after brew cycle completion) 175–205°F
- Brew temp range (comm. & home) 195–205°F

Espresso/steamed milk drinks
- Steamed milk temp. range
- Espresso brewing range

Tea steeping range
- Tea steep range 208–212°F

Legend:
- Above skin pain threshhold / Below burn damage threshold
- Above skin pain threshhold / Above burn damage threshold
- Above skin pain and burn damage thresholds / Above burn damage threshold

Acknowledgements

I sincerely appreciate the time and effort of William Charash M.D., Emergency Care, Fletcher Allen Health Care, Burlington Vermont, and David Leitner M.D., Fletcher Allen Health Care, in helping to form and edit the Burns section of this manual. Ritchie Berger, Esq. and his firm of Dinse Knapp McAndrew were indispensable in their help in shaping and editing the Brew and Sue section. I am also thankful for the edits and suggestions of Ted Lingle, former executive director of the SCAA and Coffee Quality Institute. My great appreciation is extended to my editorial assistant, Lauren Bigalow, for her indispensible assistance, research, and time. Thank you as well to Christine Hibma of Coffee Enterprises for her ongoing help and support. This publication would not have come together without the support and knowledge of these people and the Coffee Enterprises staff.

Appendix

Steam: In Context

The term "steam" refers to the vapor phase of water or the pressurized water vapor used for heating, cooking, etc.[6] This definition of steam refers to what exists in a nozzle of an espresso machine and is used to heat—steam—milk. "The steam released from the wand of an espresso machine's boiler is approximately 230 degrees Fahrenheit as it leaves the tip, although it cools rapidly as it hits room temperature air and disperses."[6] However, the term "steam" is applied in everyday life in a way that is misleading. If someone goes for a long run and it is cool outside, he might exude clouds that look like steam, but in fact, it is the visible evaporation of sweat from his body. The person "steaming" after a long run is not producing actual steam at 230°F; his sweat is simply evaporating visibly.

Comparison Temperatures

100°F-104°F: The temperature the U.S. Consumer Product Safety Commission recommends for hot tubs[45]

120°F: The temperature the U.S. Department of Energy recommends for the thermostat on home water heaters[46]

List of current warnings used on cups, lids, sleeves, and drive-thru windows

Examples of current warnings on counters or drive-thru windows:

　　CAUTION: Coffee, Tea, and Hot Chocolate are served VERY HOT.

Examples of current warnings on cups:

　　Careful, the beverage you're about to enjoy is extremely hot.

　　CAUTION: HOT CONTENTS

　　CAUTION: HANDLE WITH CARE I'M HOT

　　CAUTION: THIS BEVERAGE IS EXTREMELY HOT.

　　CAUTION: VERY HOT

　　CAUTION: HOT

Examples of current warnings on lids:

　　WARNING HOT!

　　CAUTION! CONTENTS HOT!

　　CAUTION CONTENTS HOT

　　CAUTION I'M HOT

　　CAUTION HOT

Recommended Question Topics for the Plaintiff

Questions regarding:

- The Plaintiff's assumption of the risk
- The Plaintiff's prior preparation/purchase/consumption of hot beverages, both at home and in a commercial setting
- The Plaintiff's personal knowledge that coffee (or other) beverages are generally hot
- The Plaintiff's behaviors on the day of the incident

Recommended Question Topics for the Expert Witness for the Defense:

- The expert witness's background, and background in coffee and hot beverages
- Coffee industry standards and studies

Recommended Resources:

Ted R. Lingle, *The Coffee Brewing Handbook: a Systematic Guide to Coffee Preparation*. Long Beach, CA: Specialty Coffee Association of America, 1996. Print.

M. O'Mahony, S. Pipatsattayanuwong, H. S. Lee, and S. F. Lau. *A Suitable Temperature for Serving Coffee*. Rep. Print.

H.S. Lee and M. O'Mahony, (2002), *At What Temperatures Do Consumers Like to Drink Coffee?*: Mixing Methods. Journal of Food Science, 67: 2774–2777. doi: 10.1111/j.1365-2621.2002.tb08814.x

Don Holly, *Espresso Lab: Student Manual*. Specialty Coffee Association of America, 2009. Print.

Burns – First Aid[47,] Staff, Mayo Clinic. *"Burns: First Aid - MayoClinic. com."* Mayo Clinic. Web. 20 July 2010. http://www.mayoclinic.com/health/first-aid-burns/FA00022

Jack V. Matson, *Effective Expert Witnessing*. Boca Raton: Lewis, 1994. Print.

Jim Dedman, "The Stella Liebeck McDonald's Hot Coffee Case FAQ." Web log post. *Abnormal Use: An Unreasonably Dangerous Products Liability Blog.* N.p., 25 Jan. 2011. Web. 17 Nov. 2012. <http://abnormaluse.com/2011/01/stella-liebeck-mcdonalds-hot-coffee.html>.

And Now the Rest of the Story…The McDonald's Coffee Lawsuit Kevin G. Cain, "The McDonald's Coffee Lawsuit," *Journal of Consumer & Commercial Law*

Expert witnesses in past hot beverage spill cases:

Dan Cox
Owner of Coffee Enterprises
Burlington, Vt.

Ted Lingle
Executive Director Specialty Coffee Association of America (SCAA), Retired
Executive Director Coffee Quality Institute (CQI), Retired
Long Beach, Calif.

Works Cited

1. Proceedings of A National Coffee Burn-Spill Seminar, May 21, 1999, Chicago, IL. Specialty Coffee Association of America, 1999.

2. Ted R. Lingle, *The Coffee Brewing Handbook: A Systematic Guide to Coffee Preparation* (Long Beach, CA: Specialty Coffee Association of America, 1996).

3. *Coffee Brewing Workshop Manual: Publication 54.* (New York: Coffee Brewing Center of the Pan-American Coffee Bureau, Revised 1974).

4. Pipatsattayanuwong, S., H.S. Lee, and M. O'Mahony. "Hedonic R-Index Measurement of Temperature Preferences For Drinking Black Coffee." *Journal of Sensory Studies* 16.5 (2001): 517-36.

5. H. S. Lee and M. O'Mahony, (2002), At What Temperatures Do Consumers Like to Drink Coffee?: Mixing Methods. *Journal of Food Science*, 67: 2774–2777. doi: 10.1111/j.1365-2621.2002.tb08814.x

6. Lee, Hye-Seong, E. Carstens, and M. O'Mahony. "Drinking Hot Coffee: Why Doesn't It Burn the Mouth?" *Journal of Sensory Studies* 18.1 (2003): 19-32.

7. Andrea Illy and Rinantonio Viani, eds. *Espresso Coffee: the Chemistry of Quality.* London: Academic, 1995.

8. Don Holly, *Espresso Lab: Student Manual* (Specialty Coffee Association of America, 2009).

9. Schaerer, *Schaerer Ambiente*-1 SUSA User Manual (Long Beach: Schaerer USA Corporation).

10. BUNN, *BUNN Tea Basics: Steeping a Flawless Infusion* (Springfield, IL: BUNN-O-MATIC Corporation, 2009).

11. Rancilio. *Rancilio: 10USB Technical Sheet.* Woodridge, IL: Rancilio North America Inc. PDF.

12. FETCO. *User's Guide: CBS-5000 Series Coffee Brewers.* Lake Zurich, IL: Food Equipment Technologies, 2006.

13. Wilbur Curtis Company, Inc. *Service Manual, D1000GT & D500GT Airpot Brewers.* Montebello, CA: Wilbur Curtis.

14. BUNN. *C, CT, CWTF Series Including DV, APS/TC/TS, Single CW & Twins: Operating Manual.* Springfield, IL: BUNN-O-MATIC Corporation, 2008.

15. A. R. Mortiz, and F. C. Henriques, "Studies of Thermal Injury II. The Relative Importance of Time and Surface Temperature in the Causation of Cutaneous Burns." *The American Journal of Pathology* 23.5 (1947): 695-720.

16. Jane B. Reece and Neil A. Campbell, Campbell Biology. Boston: Benjamin Cummings / Pearson Education, 2011.

17. "Burn Care 101." Burn Free. N.p., n.d. Web. 17 Nov. 2012. http://burnfree. com/Burn-Care-101.

18. Paul S. Auerbach, *Wilderness Medicine*, 5th ed. "Types of Burns." MD Consult. MD Consult, 2007. Web. 6 Aug. 2010. http://www.mdconsult.com/books/page.do?eid=4-u1.0-B978-1-4377-1678-8..00013-1--s0020&isbn=978-1-4377-1678-8&sid=1406461441&uniqId=402207585-196#4-u1.0-B978-1-4377-1678-8..00013-1--s0020.

19. John L. Hunt, Gary F. Purdue, Patrick H. Pownell, and Rod J. Rohrich, "Burns: Acute Burns, Burn Surgery, and Postburn Reconstruction." *Selected Readings in Plastic Surgery* 8.12. Web.

20. Pierrot-Deseiligny, Emmanuel, David C. Burke, and David J. Burke. "Withdrawal Reflexes." *The Circuitry of the Human Spinal Cord: Spinal and Corticospinal Mechanisms of Movement*. 2nd ed. N.p.: Cambridge UP, 2012.

21. Brown, Fredericka, and Kenneth R. Diller. "Calculating the Optimum Temperature for Serving Hot Beverages." BURNS 34 (2007): 648-54. *ScienceDirect*. Web. 20 July 2010.

22. Angelina McMahon, et al. v. BUNN-O-MATIC Corporation et al. United States District Court for the Northern District of Indiana, South Bend Division. Print.

23. Rosalind Holowaty and Boris Holowaty, Plaintiffs, v. McDonald's, Corporation and McRick, Inc., Defendants. Civil No. 4-96-925 (JRT/RLE) United States District Court for the District of Minnesota 10 F. Supp. 2d 1078; 1998 U.S. Dist. LEXIS 11102; CCH Prod. Liab. Rep. P15,317. July 13, 1998, Decided

24. Wendy A. Rogers, Nina Lamson, and Gabriel K. Rousseau. "Warning Research: An Integrative Perspective." *Human Factors* 42.1 (2000): 102-39. Web.

25. American National Standards Institute, Inc. *American National Standard for Hazardous Industrial Chemicals - Precautionary Labeling*. New York, NY: American National Standards Institute, 2006. ANSI Z129.1-2006.

26. "Smart Lid - Disposable Color Changing Coffee Cup Lids," *Smart Lid Active Beverage Packaging*. N.p., n.d. Web. 17 Nov. 2012. http://www.smartlid.com/.

27. David W. Stewart and Ingrid M. Martin, "Intended and Unintended Consequences of Warning Messages: A Review and Synthesis of Empirical Research." *Journal of Public Policy & Marketing* 13.1 (1994): 1-19. Web.

28. Jim Dedman, "The Stella Liebeck McDonald's Hot Coffee Case FAQ." Web log post. *Abnormal Use: An Unreasonably Dangerous Products Liability Blog*.

N.p., 25 Jan. 2011. Web. 17 Nov. 2012. http://abnormaluse.com/2011/01/
stella-liebeck-mcdonalds-hot-coffee.html.

29. *Hot Coffee*, Dir. Susan Saladoff. HBO, 2011. DVD.

30. "Frivolous." *Legal Information Institute*. Cornell University Law School, 19
    Aug. 2010. Web. 25 February 2013. <www.law.cornell.edu/wex/frivolous>.

31. "Products Liability." *Legal Information Institute*. Cornell University Law
    School, 19 Aug. 2010. Web. 25 February 2013. <www.law.cornell.edu/wex/
    products_liability>.

32. "Negligence." *Legal Information Institute*. Cornell University Law School,
    19 Aug. 2010. Web. 25 February 2013. <http://www.law.cornell.edu/wex/
    negligence>.

33. "Strict Liability." *Legal Information Institute*. Cornell University Law School,
    19 Aug. 2010. Web. 25 February 2013. <http://www.law.cornell.edu/wex/
    strict_liability>.

34. "Implied Warranty of Fitness." *Legal Information Institute*. Cornell University
    Law School, 19 Aug. 2010. Web. 25 February 2013. <www.law.cornell.edu/
    wex/implied_warranty_of_fitness>.

35. "Implied Warranty of Merchantibility." *Legal Information Institute*. Cornell
    University Law School, 19 Aug. 2010. Web. 25 February 2013. <http://
    www.law.cornell.edu/wex/implied_warranty_of_merchantibility>.

36. "Res Ipsa Loquitur." *Legal Information Institute*. Cornell University Law
    School, 19 Aug. 2010. Web. 25 February 2013. <www.law.cornell.edu/wex/
    res_ipsa_loqiutor>.

37. Jack V. Matson, *Effective Expert Witnessing*. Boca Raton: Lewis, 1994.

38. Sara Huppe et al., Plaintiffs, v. Twenty-First Century Restaurants of Amer-
    ica, Inc., Defendant [NO NUMBER IN ORIGINAL] Supreme Court of
    New York, Broome County.130 Misc. 2d 736; 497 N.Y.S.2d 306; 1985 N.Y.
    Misc. LEXIS 3269. January 16, 1985

39. Helen Lamkin and George Lamkin, Plaintiffs v. Braniff Airlines, Inc., De-
    fendant. Civil Action No. 87-422-RCL. United States District Court for the
    District of Massachusetts. 853 F. Supp. 30; 1994 U.S. Dist. LEXIS 7048;
    CCH Prod. Liab. Rep. P14,024. May 26, 1994, Decided

40. Christopher Nadel et al. Plaintiffs-Appellants, v. Burger King Corporation
    and Emil, Inc., Defendants-Appellees. Appeal No. C-960489. Court of Ap-
    peals of Ohio, First Appellate District, Hamilton County. 119 Ohio App. 3d
    578; 695 N.E.2d 1185; 1997 Ohio App. LEXIS 2144. May 21, 1997, Date of
    Judgment Entry On Appeal May 21, 1997, Filed

41. Angelina and Jack McMahon, Plaintiffs-Appellants, v. Bunn-O-Matic Corporation, James River Paper Company, and Wincup Holdings, L.P., Defendants-Appellees. No. 97-4131 United States Court of Appeals for the Seventh Circuit. 150 F.3d 651; 1998 U.S. App. LEXIS 14926; CCH Prod. Liab. Rep. P15,298May 27, 1998, Argued. July 2, 1998, Decided

42. Deborah Wurtzel, Plaintiff, v. Starbucks Coffee Company, Defendants. (01-CV-0324) (TCP) (MLO) United States District Court for the Eastern District of New York. 257 F. Supp. 2d 520; 2003 U.S. Dist. LEXIS 6158 April 11, 2003, Decided

43. Rachel Moltner, Plaintiff, v. Starbucks Coffee Company a/k/a Starbucks Corporation, Defendant. 08 Civ. 9257 (LAP) United States District Court for the Southern District of New York 2009 U.S. Dist. LEXIS 101413. October 23, 2009, Decided October 23, 2009, Filed

44. Gerald D. Colbert v. Sonic Restaurants, Inc. and their unknown insurer. Civil No. 09-1423 United States District Court for the Western District of Louisiana, Shreveport Division 741 F. Supp. 2d 764; 2010 U.S. Dist. LEXIS 99186 September 21, 2010, Decided September 21, 2010, Filed

45. Consumer Products Safety Commission. (1996). CPSC Issues Warning for Pools, Spas, and Hot Tubs [News release #96139]. Retrieved from http://www.cpsc.gov/en/Newsroom/News-Releases/1996/CPSC-Issues-Warning-for-Pools-Spas-and-Hot-Tubs-/

46. "Water Heating." *Energy.gov.* U.S. Department of Energy, 2 May 2012. Web. 17 Nov. 2012. http://energy.gov/energysaver/articles/tips-water-heating.

47. Staff, Mayo Clinic. "Burns: First Aid - MayoClinic.com." *Mayo Clinic.* Web. 20 July 2010. http://www.mayoclinic.com/health/first-aid-burns/FA00022.

About the Author

Dan Cox is president and owner of Coffee Enterprises (CE), located in Burlington, Vermont. CE is the administrative body for two subsidiary companies: Coffee Extracts & Ingredients (CE&I) and Coffee Analysts (CA). CE&I develops and produces coffee extracts and concentrates for leading dairy, beverage, and confectionery manufacturers. CA analyzes coffee in all forms (green, roasted, instant, and liquid) and maintains extensive physical and sensorial testing labs. Dan also acts as a consultant for strategic management and as an expert in coffee litigation cases.

Dan is a leading authority on the Specialty Coffee Industry and brings to bear thirty years of practical experience in management, roasting, cupping, product development, and marketing. Dan has written for numerous trade journals and has been a guest in many consumer media venues including *Good Morning America*, Fox News, National Public Radio, *USA Today*, *Business Week*, the *Chicago Tribune*, the *Seattle Times*, and the *Boston Herald*. From 1984 to1987 Dan was elected to three consecutive terms as national co-chairman of the Specialty Coffee Association of America, and was elected again from 1998 to 1999 as secretary/treasurer. Dan continues to be a featured speaker at its annual convention. In 2007, Dan was the second American to pass Coffee Quality Institute's rigorous Q Grader exam and is one of 239 Q Graders in the USA and one of over 2,000 worldwide.

Dan has led coffee groups on three tours of nine coffee-growing regions in Africa, Central America, Hawaii, and Jamaica. Through his work published in numerous trade and consumer journals and public presentations, he is nationally known as a resource for coffee information and trends.

Dan is the founder and president of Grounds for Health, a non-profit organization bringing healthcare to women in coffee-producing countries. To date, more than 40,000 women have been screened for cervical cancer through this program.

In 2012, Dan received the prestigious honor of Lifetime Achievement Award from the Specialty Coffee Association of America (SCAA), and was elected to the Norwich University Athletic Hall of Fame.

Along the way, Dan has served as an infantry captain in the Army, worked as an emergency medical technician, and has been elected a justice of the peace.

Contributors

Editorial and Research Assistant

Lauren Bigalow has worked in the coffee industry as a barista for six years, and was involved in training and quality control for the cafés at Cornell Dining at Cornell University. She interned at Coffee Enterprises, Inc., and learned about the coffee industry: coffee's progress from farm to cup as well as how to cup coffee. Lauren also works for Coffee Enterprises researching hot beverage litigation. She graduated from Cornell University cum laude with a BA in psychology. Currently, she resides in Shelburne, Vermont, where she makes delicious and safe coffee drinks for Village Wine and Coffee. She enjoys salsa dancing, scuba diving, and reading a book over a good cappuccino.

Photographer

Julia Luckett is a freelance photographer. She is a recent graduate of Skidmore College and holds two Bachelor of Science degrees, one in studio arts and one in music. Julia was an intern at Coffee Enterprises in the sensory department and is a lover of fine coffee. She makes a wicked latté.

Coffee Enterprises

Coffee Enterprises

Coffee Enterprises provides coffee consulting services including strategic planning, due diligence for coffee company mergers and acquisitions, coffee audits, legal consulting and testimony for coffee litigation. Coffee Enterprises also works with the investment community as well as mainstream media on all things coffee.

Coffee Analysts

Coffee Analysts

Coffee Analysts is a private, independent, SCAA certified coffee laboratory that specializes in quality assurance, product development, and specification creation of coffee and coffee-related products. Coffee Analysts conducts unbiased scientific analysis of coffee and coffee-related products and works with producers, traders, roasters, foodservice and restaurant operators, and private-label brands. By addressing practical issues from a scientific perspective, Coffee Analysts' experience provides clients with insights and information that assist in making informed decisions to manage coffee programs.

Coffee Extracts
& Ingredients

Coffee Extracts & Ingredients

Coffee Extracts & Ingredients is a purveyor of premium quality coffee products for the dairy, bakery, beverage, and confectionery industries and offers premium soluble coffee, organic coffee extracts, and fair trade coffee products.

Grounds for Health

Coffee Enterprises is proud to support Grounds for Health, an international non-profit that establishes sustainable cervical cancer prevention programs in coffee-growing countries. Coffee Enterprises President Dan Cox co-founded this non-profit organization in 1996, and has been heavily involved as a board member ever since.

CPSIA information can be obtained at www.ICGtesting.com
Printed in the USA
BVIW12n0046080615
403440BV00003B/3